How Does a Society Change?

SOCIAL
IMAGINARIES

Social Imaginaries
Series Editors:
Suzi Adams, Paul Blokker, Natalie J. Doyle, Saulius Geniusas, John W.M.
Krummel and Jeremy C.A. Smith

This ground breaking series aims to investigate social imaginaries from theoretical, comparative, historical, and interdisciplinary perspectives. Its objective is to foster challenging research on the burgeoning but heterogeneous field of social imaginaries, on the one hand, and the related field of the creative imagination, on the other. The series seeks to publish rigorous and innovative research that reflects the international, multi-regional and interdisciplinary scope across these fields.

Titles in the Series

How Does a Society Change?

Reflexivity in Politics and Education

Ingerid S. Straume

ROWMAN & LITTLEFIELD
Lanham • Boulder • New York • London

Published by Rowman & Littlefield
An imprint of The Rowman & Littlefield Publishing Group, Inc.
4501 Forbes Boulevard, Suite 200, Lanham, Maryland 20706
www.rowman.com

British Library Cataloguing in Publication Information Available

Library of Congress Cataloging-in-Publication Data

Names: Straume, Ingerid S., author.
Title: How does a society change? : Reflexivity in politics and education /
  by Ingerid S. Straume.
Description: Lanham, Maryland : Rowman & Littlefield, [2023] | Series:
  Social imaginaries | Includes bibliographical references and index. |
  Summary: "How Does a Society Change? is a scholarly work about factors
  and ideas that either facilitate or hinder social renewal and political
  change. This question is explored via original examples and conceptual
  analyses, resulting in an appeal for apprizing education and politics in
  the fullest sense of the terms"-- Provided by publisher.
Identifiers: LCCN 2022059298 (print) | LCCN 2022059299 (ebook) | ISBN
  9781786611529 (cloth : acid-free paper) | ISBN 9781786611536 (epub)
Subjects: LCSH: Education--Political aspects. | Democracy and education.
Classification: LCC LC71 .S85 2023 (print) | LCC LC71 (ebook) | DDC
  379--dc23/eng/20230201
LC record available at https://lccn.loc.gov/2022059298
LC ebook record available at https://lccn.loc.gov/2022059299

♾️™ The paper used in this publication meets the minimum requirements of
American National Standard for Information Sciences—Permanence of Paper
for Printed Library Materials, ANSI/NISO Z39.48-1992.

For Emil, Jakob, Ludvik, and Vilde.

~

Contents

~

Acknowledgements

Working across academic disciplines means to permanently be on the side. All the more important, then, is to meet people who are generous enough to include you in their scholarly community. I would like to extend my sincere thanks to those who have believed in me and my work through shifting times and across intellectual paths.

Many thanks to the editors of the Social Imaginaries book series for inviting me into this important project, and to Suzi Adams in particular for her friendly and dedicated encouragement over many years. Not only has she created an impressive body of scholarly work, but also, together with associates, built and cultivated a new scholarly field and community. A very special thanks to Johann Pàll Arnason, who has inspired, supported and generously shared his work with me, and to Peter Wagner, whose well-placed words ("she will do very well") carried me through the arduous process of writing alone during a pandemic. I also want to give thanks to Arne Johan Vetlesen, whose intellectual encouragement has helped me find my place inside a field with no name, where critical theory meets new and urgent concerns for the future; and to numerous younger colleagues and students in Greece, Norway, and elsewhere for involving me in their political enthusiasm.

Warm thanks are also due to Paul Blokker, whose gentle and precise advice has guided me from the project's inception through the final revisions, and Deni Remsberg and Katherine Harnisch at Rowman & Littlefield for invaluable, practical support. Thank you, Abdul Rahman, for sharing an invaluable story, and Unni Rustad for facilitating. But most of all, I want to thank Asgeir Olden for his steady backing and enthusiasm over the years, and not least, my dear family for all their humour and kindness.

~

Introduction

Political-Educational Questioning

There was a time when conservatives and radicals might disagree about whether or not society should be changed, and both sides could be said to have valid viewpoints. Today this question lies behind us, as the earth system's limits for a safe operating space for humanity are transgressed, one by one.[1] In 2022, Earth Overshoot Day fell on 28 July. On this date, the biological resources that can be regenerated within a year were used up. The truth of the science is hard: remaining neutral toward the present global development is no longer defensible. Human existence on the planet is unsustainable, and social change is needed. The main question from here on is how.

The aim of this book is to open up a space for questioning the social institution under current, neoliberal conditions. With regard to the more politically oriented readers, my aim is to highlight how educational perspectives extend from, and enrich, political concerns and analyses to a point where social change becomes feasible. For practitioners and scholars of education, my hope is to open up a conceptual horizon where educational matters can be recognised for their deeply political, constitutive role in how societies are instituted and how they change. Political and educational questioning are, in this analysis, two sides of the same social-historical process of self-institution.

By setting up this analogy I am not suggesting that the two theoretical domains – politics and education – have an equal status in the academic world; on the contrary, educational questions and theories have, through late modernity, been treated as rather inferior to political thought.[2] Yet, as I will argue in some detail, to ignore the inherently political nature of education –

and the educational side of politics – is in itself a political act that obscures the imaginary capacity of societies' self-institution. A central dimension of this capacity is related to the notion of political commonality, or more precisely, the realisation that the resources for individuals' political action are in, and of, the social. However, seeing that the forces that are currently driving most of the world's countries in a neoliberal direction *depend* on *obscuring* their own political-ideological historicity and social origin, this negligence is far from innocent. For neoliberal power structures, being oligarchic in essence, persist by upholding a depoliticised representation of society where social and economic structures are occulted, leaving visible only *individuals* acting, allegedly, according to their own, free choice in open (meritocratic) competition supported by market mechanisms.

My use the term 'neoliberalism' here is similar to Wendy Brown's analysis in *Undoing the Demos: Neoliberalism's Stealth Revolution*, namely, as a near-dominant governing rationality whose main effect has been to refashion other forms of rationality into economic terms. As Brown observes, neoliberal transformations affect "vocabularies, principles of justice, political culture, habits of citizenship, practices of rule, and above all, democratic imaginaries." Brown's main concern, which I fully share, is the near-totalising effects of neoliberalism on political democracy. Ubiquitous in "statecraft and the workplace, in jurisprudence, education, culture, and a vast range of quotidian activity," she notes, neoliberal reason is "converting the distinctly *political* character, meaning, and operation of democracy's constituent elements into *economic* ones."[3]

The distinctly political character of democracy is also my main concern here. In a democracy, where people are supposed to rule themselves, exposing power structures and opening them up for political questioning is essential – and a central task for democratic education. Importantly, I argue that to ignore the many connections between education and politics means to neutralise, or at least weaken, society's capacity for deliberate, political change. Through collective reflections upon what a proper education might mean, and what it should realise, a society not only questions its own, instituted meaning but also opens up for its own creative capacity. Indeed, it seems to me that the core crisis – and the core of many crises – of Western societies today is their inability to respond adequately to their own predicaments, which means to transform their own, ecologically and socially unsustainable institutions. Clear symptoms of this *crisis of the social imagination* are on display, for example, when young people raise lawsuits against their own states for not taking action to protect the environment for future generations,[4] or when young people decline to have children for similar reasons.

In a democracy, education entails a certain kind of (political) responsibility for the common world that is passed on from one generation to the next. Hannah Arendt, one of the most powerful political thinkers of the 20th century, alludes to this idea when stating that "[a]nyone who refuses to have joint responsibility for the world should not have children and must not be allowed to have part in educating them."[5] As a democratic collective, we are all responsible for furthering a type of education that assures, as far as possible, that the coming generations have opportunities not only for survival, but also for self-institution and freedom to create their own visions for living well. Democratic forms of education make social and political phenomena *matter* because the activity of forming young minds require that we need to *justify* everything we do. Through the activities of educating others, then, we assume a *de facto* responsibility for our world and our doings, even if we are not always explicit about it. Whether a society is democratic, autocratic, traditional or totalitarian, education is a central concern: to ignore education in a democracy would mean to part with self-governance, but nor can a totalitarian regime afford to disregard its educational system, which it needs to keep under total control. However, what counts as 'education' is not the same in the two cases – and indeed, as I shall argue, only the first counts as an education worthy of the name.

On this note, it is interesting to observe how educational theories tend to mirror the socio-historical reflexivity of their time, or the degree of politicisation if you like. For the question of what education means – what it *is* and what it *ought* to be – often becomes more pressing during times of social transformation and unrest. Societies that engage explicitly in their own re-organisation are actively questioning and reimagining themselves at several levels including educational theory. Indeed, as I will argue, education is one of the few social practices where institutions and subjectivity are brought into direct contact with each other, which means that social relationships, significations and traditions are constantly produced, experienced and negotiated inside its domain of practice.

A reflexive (democratic) society asks itself not only what *is* our tradition but what *ought* our tradition realise? What characterises *this* society and its current education, and what *ought* to be our aims and approaches for the future? These are political-educational questions par excellence. Of course, not all educational theories aim toward reflexive self-institution; where some educational theories are actively questioning their own foundations and aiming at social transformation, others are oriented mainly toward social re-production and the transmission of traditional ideals or values. The question for neoliberal societies – which include most of the world's countries today, many of which are authoritarian – is to what extent they are even capable of such self-reflexive questioning.

Conceptual Considerations

Education, as I see it here, is not a function of the political system but constitutive of it. Before we start to explore the intricacies of this relationship, however, some conceptual clarifications are needed. First of all, the concept of education brought into play here comes with certain – unavoidable – linguistic challenges. The problem stems from the fact that I am writing from the university discipline called *pädagogik* in the Scandinavian languages and German, referring both to a discipline and a concept that lack English correlates. Unlike the English term 'pedagogy,' which denotes a practice, notably methods of teaching, *pädagogik* circumscribes a rather broad, scholarly field whose perspectives are cultural, historical and often critical. Pädagogik is a *Wissenschaft* – a field of knowledge, not a science – established during the 18th century and later consolidated into four, modern subdisciplines: the philosophy, history, psychology and sociology of education. The dominant 'knowledge interest' of modern *pädagogik*, to say it with Jürgen Habermas, is *emancipation*. From here on I will, as far as possible, use the term 'education' to refer this broader, cultural meaning of *pädagogik* and otherwise use *schooling* or other terminology. A more detailed discussion of the term 'education' can be found in chapter 3.

A second conceptual consideration concerns the term 'politics,' which also holds a range of different meanings. A good place to start is French political theory, with philosopher, political thinker and psychoanalyst Cornelius Castoriadis's definition of politics as questioning – "the explicit putting into question" – of "the established institution of society."[6] This kind of political activity, according to philosopher, sociologist and historian Marcel Gauchet, is concerned with society as a whole, not just with competing interests between individuals or groups. In order to think politically, Gauchet argues, a conception of the social institution as a *unity* is needed.[7] In other words, as long as we are thinking in terms of the interests or needs of individuals or groups, we are not really thinking politically. There is of course a risk here of overlooking the historical fact that progressive political developments – including work regulations, welfare arrangements, liberties and rights – are the concrete results of specific struggles such as the workers' movements fighting for their interests; but the idea is that political creation, such as making laws and constitutions, has the good of the society as a whole as its object.

In this respect, a better term than *unity* could be Christian Laval and Francis Vergne's notion of democratic *commonality*.[8] My point, which will hopefully become clearer in the chapters to come, is that attention to (conceptions of) society as a unity or political commonality can help us distinguish the *lack* of political thought in neoliberal rationality and to withstand tendencies to subsume political categories under other, pre-political, domains.[9]

The concept of politics used here shares with education the orientation toward an emancipatory knowledge interest. A further distinction that is central for what I have called political-educational questioning can be drawn between 'politics' and 'the political.' This distinction – deployed by Castoriadis, Gauchet, Laval and other French thinkers – will be discussed in detail later. For now, let me say that there is a type of *doubleness* at play in my examination whereby certain concepts – such as education and politics – bear in them a potential for self-reflexiveness and self-questioning. This structural similarity – i.e., how both concepts can be reflexive/non-reflexive – may be tentatively formulated as a parallel: as 'politics' relates to 'the political,' so 'education' relates to 'schooling'; and both are expressions of how the *instituting* relates to the *instituted* society. This line of reasoning is strongly influenced by Cornelius Castoriadis, author of *The Imaginary Institution of Society*, who is one of the few thinkers that have devoted themselves to exploring what a society is, and how a society creates, upholds and changes itself. As I hope to demonstrate, then, attention to these concepts' doubleness is necessary (or at least very helpful) for a society's explicit self-questioning because they engage with the capacities for self-institution that characterise the historical *project of autonomy*.[10]

So far, I have pointed out some structural similarities and connections between education and politics. However, the question of education, what it is and what it ought to be, is rarely at the forefront of political and social theory. Nonetheless I find it to be implicit, or just below the surface of many of my favourite thinkers: Cornelius Castoriadis, Hannah Arendt, Axel Honneth, Charles Taylor, and behind these, Hegel and Aristotle. In the following pages I will draw on their ideas and theories to explore the notion of society's self-reflexive (political-educational) questioning and use elements from their conceptual apparatuses along with historical and contemporary examples to establish an understanding of the political meaning of education and vice versa.

The level of analysis in this book is conceptual and historical, rather than oriented toward the "realities of the classroom." This may sound odd, coming from a philosopher of education: Should not the student, or the child, be the most important factor in an education worthy of its name? I have my reasons

– many reasons – to go beyond what is ordinarily considered the domain of an educational theory, such as didactics, teaching, learning and relationships. One of them is to withstand the pressure for depoliticisation: For there is already a danger in educational studies to limit the focus to individual subjects, especially under today's neoliberal regime where individuals' ability to learn and perform is the overarching political credo that occults structural levels, including the imaginary dimensions of the political. Another reason, related to the first, is that I find that the most interesting theory development takes place at the level of the social imaginary.

One of the most acute problems with what passes as education today is how big-tech corporations target individuals in the name of personal adaptation and freedom of choice, while in effect reducing them to data-generating entities.[11] Whether a child's subjectivity should be formed by corporations and agents beyond democratic control or by educators following a public/democratic mandate seems to me a political question of the deepest, most critical importance. Processes where small children – who are social, intelligent beings ready for attachment and love – are separated and set to compete against each other from an early age are not only destructive to their subjective self-formation but also to the notion of commonality, so important to democratic politics.[12] For politics is not only about debating in parliament or handling public affairs; it concerns our common institutions, arrangements and imaginaries.[13] In Hannah Arendt's words,

> The polis, properly speaking, is not the city-state in its physical location; it is the organization of the people as it arises out of acting and speaking together, and its true space lies between people living together for this purpose, no matter where they happen to be.[14]

In order to create this kind of polis – where attention to public affairs cultivates what we have in common – institutions and collective arrangements are needed. Another evocative image to describe this dimension can be found in Arendt's description of a public, common world. "To live together in the world," she states, "means essentially that a world of things is between those who have it in common, as a table is located between those who sit around it; the world, like every in-between, relates and separates men at the same time."[15] Keeping the political realm vividly alive means to foster a space for public questioning open, materially and in the collective imagination. The metaphor also illustrates how people occupy and speak from *different* positions in the world: When sharing viewpoints across a table, we may learn from each other's perspectives while making them public and in that sense common.

The Nordic Outlook

Over the past years, a great number of scholars have analysed how a neo-liberal world-order is transforming political landscapes, social relationships and professional conditions. How these transformations unfold depends on contextual – geographical and sociocultural – trajectories, but some general observations can be asserted, including the relocation of industry, deregulation, rising inequalities and big-tech capitalism. I have tried to balance my presentation, but it seems unavoidable that the US becomes a point of reference in these – and other – respects. The main reason is that their literature is more influential (due to accessibility and language), but also because their examples of neoliberal transformations are sometimes more extreme and the developments of concern more accentuated.

Other forms of bias are even more difficult to overcome. Although this book is not about Scandinavian education or politics, its point of outlook is definitely Northern Europe. In this region where Protestant ethics, pietism and social democracy have prevailed, an explicit political aim has been to level social classes through public education. Education of the common people, peasants, also played a central part in the development of modern Nordic nation-states and parliamentarism.[16] The Nordic educational systems – with Sweden increasingly as an anomaly – are overwhelmingly public; schools normally follow a national curriculum; and education, including the higher levels, is free of charge.[17]

One of the characteristics of students in the Nordic region is their enduringly high score in school surveys of 'democratic citizenship' such as the International Civic and Citizen Education Study of the International Association for the Evaluation of Educational Achievement (IEA).[18] Of course, parameters used in these studies, such as environmental sustainability and gender equality, are valued explicitly in Nordic education – and they are also part of the normative framework here. For example, living with a strong welfare-state system, I find it difficult to understand why many Americans are critical of publicly funded health services or why parents should decide which books should be allowed in school libraries. A certain Eurocentrism will certainly colour my discussions along with other forms of bias such as 'white privilege'.

Scandinavian *pädagogik* has historically been progressive, child-centred and socially inclusive with a strong foothold in critical theory, especially in the period 1975–1990, before the neoliberal era had settled in. During the 20th century the centre of orientation for Nordic schools and universities gradually shifted from Germany toward the Anglo-American sphere, and with this, from a self-understanding based on *Wissenschaft* and scholarship to *science* and *research*. A major stakeholder in this transition has been the OECD (Organisation for Economic Co-operation and Development), which, along with the EU, has decisively shaped public policies and educational institutions. The shift in geographical orientation from continental Europe to the US, complemented by a technocratic turn in policy and research, has led to a new orientation toward measurement and testing which represents a major shift in self-understanding across the public sector and its professions. This *neoliberal reorientation* – which is taking place across the world – has probably diminished some of the regional differences in orientation and scholarly traditions, but far from all.

One of the keys to understanding how the Nordic region, which consists of the three Scandinavian countries, Finland, and Iceland, became a relatively peaceful and stable part of the world with persistently high scores on parameters such as welfare, social mobility, equality and well-being, can be found in how conflicts between social groups have been settled in the past. The Nordic welfare states were developed via political struggles where conflicts were explicitly settled through mediating institutional arrangements such as collective bargaining.[19] The relative equality, trust in authorities and aspirations to full employment that characterise these states were thus founded on the open recognition that a society consists of conflicting interests, notably between labour and capital, and that these conflicting interests need to be mediated in institutions.[20]

The Northern European reorientation from Germany to the US, and more generally the tendency to import influential theories that carry with them assumptions about everything from notions of state power to justice, comes with certain risks. Among these are difficulties in understanding one's own regional context. As a case in point, consider the concept of democratic citizenship (the theme of a later chapter), where the available literature is largely from the Anglo-American sphere. The dominant notion of citizenship in the Nordic region is, according to political historian Pauli Kettunen, a form of 'social citizenship' where individuals are engaged as parties in social relationships based on their *interests*.[21] This competition stands in contrast to the emphasis of individuals' social *rights* that characterises Anglo-American accounts.[22] One of the fundamental differences between the Nordic region and most other countries in the world is how the relationship between individuals and the state in the Nordic context is characterised by a high degree of trust in the (benevolence of the) state. Accordingly, when Anglo-American political theory, rooted in very different historical experiences, is imported to Nordic university departments, the need for historical and critical awareness is needed. Indeed, Kettunen argues, the new focus on individual rights in Nordic academia and society could become a source of new social conflicts and distrust between groups.

A similar argument can be made for the (Anglo-American) ideology of meritocracy, where individuals are believed to rise to their merited position via their talents and educational efforts. This seemingly harmless belief becomes politically potent when bolstered by the neoliberal credo that individual subjects are *responsible* for whatever happens to them through their *choices* – a notion that occults notions of collective interests and public responsibility while pushing individuals and groups into a more fragmented and polarised state, where educational merit becomes an instrument for social stratification.[23] When new meritocratic beliefs are combined with a certain Nordic tendency to smugness – believing that they are still among the best nations to live in, and mistaking their luck for merit – these countries may become more vulnerable to neoliberal onslaughts. For despite the Nordic nations' history of valuing solidarity, equity and inclusion, their political culture or institutions have not been able to maintain equality in wealth and income – indeed, although still below the OECD average, the increase of inequality (measured as equivalised disposable incomes) in the Nordics is among the largest in the OECD area.[24]

Finally, a few words about normative orientation. When new children are brought into the world, adults become parents and educators, which often means that they assume responsibility for taking out the best in themselves and to consider what elements of their traditions are seen as worthy of passing on to the next generation. There are probably almost as many opinions about what the most important questions of our time are as there are subjects who can ask and question. For my part, two of the most important questions are: What are the conditions for bringing up a child in or toward freedom, today? And what may we hope for, in terms of the future of human and non-human life on the planet?

Chapters Outline

Education can represent a window for individual self-realisation or a brutal hierarchy with winners and losers. Chapter 1 offers some examples of both from various parts of the world. The main part of the chapter provides a background for understanding how education during the 20th century became a matter of investment in a global competition for economic dominance. Starting from the Cold War, I discuss how historical shifts and ambiguities in the functions of education – for example, emancipation versus schooling – can be seen as foreshadowing today's global, neoliberal regime dominated by meritocratic ideology and 'big tech' capital. The notion of a 'cultural cold war' illustrates how mind control – owning the winning narrative – is an important dimension in battles for geopolitical hegemony, but also how creative people have found and established pockets of resistance. The chapter closes by outlining two historically distinct conceptions of education: the Anglo-American 'curriculum tradition' emphasising methodology, individual learning and testing and the European 'bildung tradition,' where education is seen as a cultural discipline linked to emancipation and self-realisation. In effect, Cold War reforms linking the school system to the military and the global economy served to fortify the former and discredit the latter in Europe and other parts of the world and became a central forerunner for today's individualised learning technologies.

Chapter 2 continues to explore the theoretical connections between education and politics introduced here in the introduction. Building on the idea that certain concepts contain, or hold, the potential for reflexivity – a conceptual 'doubleness' – the chapter introduces Cornelius Castoriadis's theory about how the 'instituted' and the 'instituting' society are in permanent tension: a tension that can be elucidated in order to strengthen a society's capacity to change itself. This potential for social change, as I argue in some detail, is occulted by neoliberal ideology. Concepts introduced in the chapter include Castoriadis's understanding of the individual, whose formative resources are always in the social; the social imaginary; autonomy and authenticity; subjectivity/intersubjectivity; and the paradox of educational authority.

In chapter 3, I take a closer look at the concept of education itself. First, I explore connections between the European concept of bildung[25] (or in Greek, *paideia*) and a notion of 'education proper' as identified by English speaking philosophers of education. I further explore how the dark twin of education proper, 'schooling,' is an important dimension of society's socialisation processes: its 'ground power' related to implicit and explicit control. The chapter also addresses the widespread tendency to reduce education to an instrument for something else. One example is the influential critique, set forth by the Dutch educational theorist Gert Biesta, of the neoliberal regime of 'learnification,' or 'learning society.' The chapter examines Biesta's position, in some detail, as the foremost spokesperson for a political conception of education, and finds that, while having some very important ambitions and critical insights, Biesta nevertheless ignores the fact that the resources for individual subjectivity are in and of social. He therefore fails to understand the relationship between particular (reflexive) forms of socialisation and subject formation. A related problem is Biesta's individualist framework, which leads him to ignore the capacity of collective questioning and the importance of institutions. Of course, Biesta is not alone in endorsing these perspectives; both shortcomings are also characteristic of a neoliberal ideology which conceals its own political imaginary.

Chapter 4 is devoted to democracy and citizenship education. Starting with the concept of democracy itself, which has many meanings and internal tensions, I devote some attention to the first notion of citizenship in Athenian democracy, where important distinctions were drawn for the first time. A central distinction from this period is – in contemporary terms – the subject position of the citizen versus the consumer representing, respectively, the public and the private domains of interest. I then turn to some of the most influential contemporary theories of citizenship and education in a democracy, viz. John Dewey's 'experimental citizen'; Amy Gutmann's (and John Rawls's) conception of education's mandate in a diverse, pluralistic society, here referred to as the 'deliberative citizen'; and Chantal Mouffe's notion of agonal citizenship, where the citizen is cast as 'adversary.' Together with Biesta (chapter 4), I conclude that each of these theorists addresses important aspects of modern, liberal democracy, but also that, compared to democracy theories with a stronger emphasis on the political dimension, there is a danger that these approaches to citizenship education fasten in questions that concern individuals or groups at the cost of elucidating larger, social structures, which today would mean fossil-driven production and the (big tech) economy: questions that concern and engage with societal change. The chapter ends with a section on populism, where I argue that regimes endorsing right-wing populism do not really value education and argue why this is among the most blatant forms of depoliticisation today.

Finally, chapter 5 takes a step into questioning the future. How can we address big-tech corporations and massive environmental degradation? And more generally, what is the proper level of political-educational questioning? Arguing that although societal change is important, yes, necessary, it seems unfair and overblown to educate every young person to become 'change agents,' as many universities today proclaim to do. Indeed, this can be seen as another turn of the neoliberal screw that overburdens the individual with responsibility while occluding social structures. Under the current circumstances, then, perhaps our educational efforts would be better spent in establishing a ground for democratic commonality, and a middle way, where what we can hope for is to live well within our planetary limits, and as part of this, to guard the project of autonomy and self-rule.

Notes

1. Stockholm Resilience Centre, https://www.stockholmresilience.org/research/planetary-boundaries.html

2. Along with the hierarchy of 'hard' versus 'soft' sciences developed during the 19th and 20th centuries, there is probably a gender aspect, where professions dealing with children and human subjectivity have generally held low status. The situation looked very different in other periods, notably in Europe during German idealism (ca. 1770–1840), when leading philosophers considered education of the soul to be most valuable and worth pondering, while political thought was associated with the military and brutish domains of human life.

3. Wendy Brown, *Undoing the Demos: Neoliberalism's Stealth Revolution* (Cambridge, MA/London: Zone Books, 2015), 17.

4. *The Guardian*, https://www.theguardian.com/environment/2021/may/07/the-young-people-taking-their-countries-to-court-over-climate-inaction

5. Hannah Arendt, "The Crisis in Education," in *Between Past and Future* (New York: Penguin, 2006), 186.

6. Cornelius Castoriadis, "Power, Politics, Autonomy," in *Philosophy, Politics, Autonomy: Essays in Political Philosophy*, ed. David Ames Curtis, 159 (New York: Oxford University Press, 1991).

7. Natalie Doyle, *Marcel Gauchet and the Loss of Common Purpose* (Lanham, MD: Lexington Books/Rowman & Littlefield, 2018).

8. Christian Laval and Francis Vergne, *Éducation Démocratique: La révolution scolaire à venir* (Paris: La Découverte, 2021).

9. For the latter argument, see James Wiley, *Politics and the Concept of the Political: The Political Imagination* (New York: Routledge, 2016) or Sheldon Wolin, *Politics and Vision: Continuity and Innovation in Western Political Thought* (Princeton, NJ: Princeton University Press, 2004).

10. Castoriadis, "Power, Politics, Autonomy."

11. Kenneth J. Saltman, "Artificial Intelligence and the Technological Turn of Public Education Privatization: In Defence of Democratic Education," *London Review of Education* 18 no. 2 (2020).

12. Laval and Vergne, *Éducation Démocratique*.

13. The term 'imaginaries' is here used more or less synonymously – and interchangeably – with Castoriadis's concept "social imaginary significations." I discuss the concepts in more detail in chapter 2.

14. Hannah Arendt, *The Human Condition* (Chicago: University of Chicago Press, 1958/1998), 198.

15. Arendt, *The Human Condition*, 52. Arendt insisted on using the term 'men' rather than, for example, 'human beings.'

16. Daniel Tröhler, "Introduction: The Nordic Education Model: Trajectories, Configurations, Challenges," in *The Nordic Education Model in Context: Historical Developments and Current Renegotiations*, ed. Tröhler et al. (London: Routledge, 2022).

17. Public services are being privatised in the Nordic region as well, especially during periods of right-liberal governments when corporations and consortia are invited into publicly funded welfare services, often generating large fortunes hidden in complex, corporate structures and tax havens.

18. IEA, https://www.iea.nl/studies/iea/iccs/2022

19. Sakari Hänninen, Kirsi-Marja Lehtelä and Paula Saikkonen (eds.), *The Relational Nordic Welfare State: Between Utopia and Ideology* (London: Edward Elgar, 2019).

20. Pauli Kettunen, "The Rise and Fall of the Nordic Utopia of an Egalitarian Wage Work Society," in *The Relational Nordic Welfare State*, ed. Hänninen et al. Another historically important factor was the political role of the peasant, whose ability to read and write was seen as central for building a parliamentary system and nation state.

21. Kettunen, "The Rise and Fall of the Nordic Utopia."

22. Work is a central category for Kettunen. He describes the development of the Nordic welfare state as an effort to "make it everybody's right to fulfil everybody's duty to work" (102).

23. Michael Sandel, *The Tyranny of Merit: What's Become of the Common Good?* (New York: Farrar, Straus and Giroux, 2020).

24. Rolf Aaberge et al., "Increasing Income Inequality in the Nordics," *Nordic Economic Policy Review 2018*, Nordic Council of Ministers.

25. In passages where the term is used in a general way, and not referring to the German Bildung tradition, bildung is spelled with a small b. See chapter 3 for more elaboration.

CHAPTER ONE

The Politics of Education

The role played by education in all political utopias from ancient times onward shows how natural it seems to start a new world with those who are by birth and nature new.

—Hannah Arendt, *The Origins of Totalitarianism*

How do societies change? And how can they *be* changed? One of the enduring questions in the human sciences relates to how societies are constituted – as institutions giving form to specific types social meaning – and how they are transformed, historically and politically. Education, as Hannah Arendt observes, is part of the answer. Since societies reproduce themselves mainly through the education of new generations, reformers eager to change existing socio-political conditions have often been spokespersons for *new* kinds of education, changing society from the ground up, so to speak. Environmental education, education for sustainability, peace education and cosmopolitan education are just a few recent examples of how education is postulated as the gateway for realising political objectives. In the most ideological cases, educational revolutionaries have aimed at creating a new type of human being with a different sociality, who in turn will be the source of new forms of social intercourse and organised power.

Faced with insurmountable challenges such as anthropogenic climate change and species extinction, it may seem easier, and safer for policymakers, to focus on the educational system with 'quality frameworks' rigged for educating 'change agents,' 'entrepreneurs' and 'cosmopolitan citizens' rather than addressing problems directly.

Realistic or not, as soon as we move from political ideals to reform or action, the question of education requires attention. This is what Aristotle underscores when stating, in *The Politics*, that the prime duty of a lawgiver is to "arrange for the education of the young." "In states where this is not done," he contends, "the quality of the constitution [*politeia*] suffers." But education cannot be the same in every type of state or regime, as Aristotle explains:

> Education must be related to the particular constitution in each case, for it is the special character appropriate to each constitution that set it up at the start and commonly maintains it, e.g., the democratic character preserves a democracy, the oligarchic an oligarchy. And in all circumstances, a better character is a cause of a better constitution.[1]

Observing that the formation of society's institutions and the formation of its individual members depend on each other, the importance of education in socio-political affairs cannot be underestimated for Aristotle. And although more pronounced in ancient than in modern social theory, the dependence of the political order on educational institutions is still valid. Accordingly, one of the first things an authoritarian regime will do to secure its power base is to seize control over the educational system Typical signs of regimes that cannot afford to ignore education are to erase, defame and delegitimise the history of their opponents. In other words, when totalitarian regimes hold their heavy hands over education, revising textbooks and indoctrinating children from an early age, their aim is not only to prevent the ability but also the very impulse to question authorities and their legitimacy. Similarly, efforts to uphold a given social order, including hierarchies and injustices, are embodied in school rituals like pledges of allegiance, national symbols like the flag, historical heroes, literary canons, songs and prayers. The shaping of young minds through *schooling* is probably the most efficient form of social power. With technologies such as personalised electronic media and advanced surveillance systems, the opportunities for such shaping have increased immensely.[2]

The alliance between education and state formation is no less important for democracies, though. As regimes of people's self-governance, democratic institutions simply cannot work without an informed (educated) and politically active citizenry. This point, undisputed in educational and political theory, is most famously expressed by John Dewey's phrase from 1916, stating that: "Democracy is more than a form of government; it is primarily a mode of associated living, of conjoint communicated experience."[3] For Dewey, a democratic society that is flexible and oriented toward growth, openness, learning and self-improvement is more sustainable than a society that is rigid and inflexible. Dewey's pragmatist conception of a liberal education is more or less the opposite of the schooling in a totalitarian setting – and in reality, only the former can be called education in the proper sense of the word. For while education is generally considered a good, the concept of schooling is more ambiguous. However, there are also some problematic sides to the most universalistic claims of what good education can achieve in an individual's life. The next section will show some examples.

An Investment in the Future

The Universal Declaration of Human Rights (UDHR) of 1948, Article 26.1 reads:

> Everyone has the right to education. Education shall be free, at least in the elementary and fundamental stages. Elementary education shall be compulsory. Technical and professional education shall be made generally available and higher education shall be equally accessible to all on the basis of merit.[4]

Even though education is recognised as a fundamental human right, the Global Education Monitoring Report from 2016 showed that 61 million children did not have access to basic education, and 758 million adults in the world were illiterate.[5] Major policy programmes, such as the United Nations Sustainability Goals, are set up to amend the global demand for education. In large parts of the world, children will walk and travel for hours and endure much hardship to attend school. For the family, keeping a child in school can be costly; yet investing in the education of at least one of its members can help the whole family to improve its condition, however slightly. Education is generally viewed as an investment in the future, for individuals, families and states – but the educational process in each case starts a long time before the person in question, the individual child, can have a say, since, according to the UDHR, parents have a "prior right to choose the kind of education that shall be given to their children."

The reason why parents can make educational choices on the child's behalf is of course that education is almost universally considered a good. But what kind of good is it? Is there more to education than becoming literate and qualified for certain types of work, securing an income and a certain status? Can we say that educational processes carry values of their own – and if so, what kind of values are they, are they the same to everyone, and are they equally accessible? And on a different yet related note, why is access to formal education, especially for girls and women, so often attacked by religious-military groups such as, currently, the Taliban (Afghanistan and Pakistan) and the Nigerian Salafist group Boko Haram? When the Pakistani Taliban attempted to execute the 15-year-old activist Malala Yousafzai for claiming girls' right to education, their fear was exposed in full. What are they so afraid of? Questions such as these quickly lead into deeper questions about power, freedom and socio-historical valuations. Clearly, there is more meaning to the notion of education than learning to read and write – even though there is power in that, too.

A possible clue can be found in the United Nations system, where the right to education is framed in rather expansive terms. Article 26 of the Universal Declaration of Human Rights, for example, boldly states that:

> Education shall be directed to the full development of the human personality and to the strengthening of respect for human rights and fundamental freedoms. It shall promote understanding, tolerance and friendship among all nations, racial or religious groups, and shall further the activities of the United Nations for the maintenance of peace.[6]

Here, a direct link is established between education and "fundamental freedoms" such as tolerance and friendship between all groups as being so many steps toward world peace. While policy programs and curricula commonly articulate educational goals in terms of *knowledge, skills* and *attitudes* – and more recently as *competences*, which contain all three dimensions – the Declaration is clearly dominated by the cultivation of attitudes. It is also saturated with the universalist language of Western liberalism. This UN jargon – with its tendency to subsume all other discourses under its pretentions, and bordering, arguably, on self-contentedness – *may* provide a key to understanding why oppressive religious groups like the Taliban are so determined to prohibit education for girls, and why Boko Haram, who harm, kidnap and abuse school children, have targeted education as the main political factor of "Western influence." Education for them is *not* a neutral good, but a value-laden effort aimed at undermining their own, tyrannical and strictly hierarchical regimes.

In August 2021, after two decades of warfare against the Taliban, US troops, followed by NATO forces, abandoned Afghanistan on ultra-short notice. During the final days of the evacuation, as the Taliban were closing in on Kabul, 20-year-old Abdul Rahman, who had recently graduated from the American University in Kabul, wrote a letter that was published in a Norwegian newspaper, looking back at his university days. "Each night after our classes," Abdul writes, "we knew a long and dangerous journey awaited us." Having dealt with armed gangs and controlled neighbourhoods, bombs, lockdowns and roadblocks, Abdul counted himself as privileged:

> Not everyone gets the chance to study in Afghanistan. And studying in a top university is a dream come true. I believed that after graduating, I could find a good job and support my family. And when sometimes I felt despondent, I would tell myself that in the next few months the war would end in Afghanistan and the situation would get much better.

Instead, the hardship kept increasing until the university itself was attacked by a group of Taliban terrorists:

> A car bomb drove near our university and exploded, shattering the south wall of our campus like glass. Armed terrorists poured into our campus and fired at anyone in sight. Some students climbed barbed wire walls to jump to safety. When the attackers got inside the buildings, students had to jump from second and third floors to a concrete ground. . . . The attackers broke the lock doors of classes and threw hand grenades to kill anyone inside. Dozens of students lost their lives, some of my friends among them. Others were badly injured. A girl who jumped from the third floor broke her back and later, after one year, came to the University in a wheelchair.

At that point, Abdul feared that his parents would not allow him to continue his studies. But instead, they encouraged him to study even harder for the sake of those students who had lost their lives:

> Despite the days with the deafening sound of bomb explosions and the long nights with the scream of sirens and the whistle of bullets, I finished my university and graduated. The night after our graduation, we had a small party to celebrate. With my friends, I talked about all the new roads that now opened for us, because we were among the few with a degree from a top university in Kabul. Little did we know that in the next few days, all these newly opened roads would be permanently closed on us.

Shortly after Abdul's graduation, the US and NATO troops withdrew from Afghanistan, and the Taliban moved in with tanks and weapons. Locked inside his family's apartment, fearing for their lives, Abdul finished his letter to the outside with the following words:

> The bright future in which I had believed and fought for is no more there. In other words, I fought for nothing. Students in our university died for nothing.

The girl who came to university in a wheelchair to study came literally for nothing.[7]

From the initial joy of being accepted at university, through struggles with interrupted studies and his parents' constant worry, to the utter disappointment of not being able to use his education for a greater good, the story of Abdul is one of hope, sacrifice, and personal investment in the belief of what higher education can do in a young person's life.

Taliban and Boko Haram are of course extreme in their efforts to eradicate the Western education that they abhor.[8] Their actions cannot be defended as freedom struggles in any meaningful way. Nonetheless, there is a background history here of Western colonialism that is shared by many people and groups across the world. For wherever there was a Western missionary, there was a school, and wherever there was a school, there was reading of books: first holy books, then school material produced by the colonial power in the colonial language with limited local relevance, often out-dated and of doubtful quality. Today, one of the most lasting effects of colonial dominance is the global use of colonial languages, especially English in secondary and higher education, a trend that is upheld and supported by neoliberal policies and corporate interests.

Colonial Education and the Rhetoric of Rising

Education, according to the UNESCO, is "one of the most powerful tools by which economically and socially marginalized children and adults can lift themselves out of poverty and participate fully in society."[9] In the UN system, education is seen as "essential for the exercise of all other human rights" as it "promotes individual freedom and empowerment" and "important development benefits."[10] And education *can* certainly be a key to economic improvement – in some cases the only key – and in the longer term a path toward equity and individual self-realisation, mobility, and liberation for women especially, as recognised in the UN's Sustainable Development Goals as well as individuals and social movements across the world demanding access to education. But education – Western or not – is not a highway leading directly into empowerment, sustainability or freedom. Indeed, for some, it can be the opposite.

It seems fair to recall that in a colonised world, 'educational' beliefs and institutions have historically been employed to undermine local and traditional customs and languages. In such cases, education, or rather, the kind of *schooling* aimed at shaping the minds of other people, ultimately means force and dominion. Colonial schooling is also the story of exploitation and dominance where so-called civilising ideas and hierarchical imaginaries have been applied to suppress, replace and uproot other (traditional) forms of meaning. Positing some words and texts as holy – as gateways to salvation from illiterate savagery – has been particularly effective in forging relations of dominion. In the early phases of formal education, very close connections were established between schools, churches, temples and mosques, and the teacher and the priest were often one and the same person. This mode of organisation underpins a hierarchy of languages and whiteness whereby the teacher represents an authority close to the god. Among the grimmest examples in the history of education is when indigenous children were taken from their parents, in country after country, Norway included, and locked up in boarding schools where their native language and customs were not only ignored but forbidden and violently 'driven out.'[11] Indeed, up until the 1970s, the school system was the central instrument of the Western world for devaluating and extinguishing traditional, non-modern forms of knowledge, with repercussions to this day.[12]

At present, a different yet related set of problems is afflicting the field of education. In a growing number of countries, entering the path of education means that children from an early age are enrolled in hard competition, a competition that sometimes lasts for life. Ambitious and affluent parents from Asia to Latin America send their children as early as the age of four to schools where the medium of instruction is a colonial language. For the rest of their school years, these children will be instructed in (a local version of) that language in the parents' hope that this will give them a head-start in life.[13] Unfortunately, serious setbacks in learning can be observed, especially for the less privileged or minority groups who do not speak or understand the language of instruction.[14]

Tanzania is one example where the negative effects of this practice have been documented for many years.[15] But despite the (research-based) efforts of the first president, Julius Nyerere, and much later John Magufuli (president 2015–2021) to make Kiswahili the language of instruction in primary and secondary school, the overwhelming majority of the Tanzanian middle class will send their children to schools where English is the medium of instruction. Parents who can afford it choose charter/church schools where English is the norm, and the most ambitious ones even converse with their offspring in English, reserving Kiswahili for purposes such as communicating with domestics. And so, as the most lasting impact of colonialism, the mother tongue with which we think and communicate, is treated as inferior and replaced with a bleak (Americanised) copy of a living language – in Tanzania, in Nepal, in Mexico and increasingly in Norway.[16] Indeed, according to educational policy researchers Deem, Mok and Lucas, a number of Asian countries have "not really 'de-colonized' in practice" but are strongly influenced by "Anglo-Saxon standards or ideologies" which shape their academic practices. The researchers observe that:

> The introduction of English as the medium of instruction, the adoption of curricula from Australia, the UK and the USA, sending home students to study overseas and establishing international exchanges, coupled with the quest for the world-class universities as predominately defined by the Anglo-Saxon world, have not only created a new 'dependency culture' but also reinforced the American-dominated 'hegemony,' particularly in relation to league tables, citation indexes and the kind of research that counts as high status.[17]

Asian societies, they argue, have treated "internationalization" as "westernization" and "Americanization." However, the biggest problem here may not be Americanisation, but rather what the authors mention in the continuation, namely *the measuring and quantifying of everything from performance to status*. As I observe in the introduction, this tendency to quantify everything human is the main attribute of an educational system subjected to neoliberal reforms whose goal is to intensify the global competition for prestige, hegemony and capital. And as if this was not enough, the pressure is further intensified by the inflation of grades and qualifications. For at the same time that education became the global remedy for almost everything – recall how former UK prime minister Tony Blair had "education, education, education" as his campaign motto – most nations broadening their educational basis have seen an inflation in the level of qualifications to the point where, according to Thomas Piketty, "a high school diploma now represents what a grade school certificate used to mean, a college degree what a high school diploma used to stand for, and so on."[18] And so the paradoxical situation is that while (higher) education is seen as an individual imperative, the only means for not "falling behind," its value in the labour market is constantly diminishing.

The social mechanism whereby individuals, just in order to keep their position, constantly need to work harder, improve and increase their efforts is vividly described by sociologist Hartmut Rosa as "dynamic stabilisation."[19] In a world marked by 'acceleration' (another concept from Rosa), where everybody feels the constant need to perform more efficiently in every sphere of life, simply keeping up and not losing one's position means to constantly struggle. Subjected to the same, competitive ideology, children across the world are continuously being drilled and trained for selective promotion in a test-driven educational system, sometimes with enormous personal costs.

Consequently, young persons, called 'students' from the age of four, undergo years of private tutoring in order to be accepted at institutions that are continuously ranked by global indices. In this system propelled by high-stakes testing and 'the rhetoric of rising' – well described by Michael Sandel in *The Tyranny of Merit* – ordinary public schooling and the language spoken by local people are considered insufficient and private tutoring essential in order to get ahead or simply to keep up. Compared to industrial child labour, begging or working on the street, even this kind of schooling is probably preferable although with costs such as shrinking the child's free time for imagination and play – and in some cases, depression, anxiety and suffering, sometimes to the point of suicide. Tragically, this is not an exaggeration.[20]

Education, then, is not a uniform thing or unambiguous good: it can both expand and narrow a person's capacities, their subjectivity, available imaginaries and possible life paths. At its best, education opens horizons of meaning, with opportunities for creativity and fulfilment – but for many there is also disappointment awaiting after graduation, as was the case for Abdul, who saw his enormous efforts as wasted when the Taliban literally closed him in. Moreover, in many countries with high enrolment in higher education, students with a bachelor or even master's degree may find themselves driving taxis as there are no relevant jobs available. During a work-related visit to Tanzania, for example, my driver told me with great frustration that all the members of his cohort studying business administration were told to become entrepreneurs at the end of their studies. This unhelpful advice is like a perfect echo of the neoliberal rationality: a rationality that, in the words of Niklas Angebauer, "promotes and enforces a bundle of regulative ideas on how to exist, behave, and flourish as a human being." Referring to a vast body of literature, he notes that "the subjectivity thereby created is distinctly entrepreneurial; for it is the entrepreneur who figures as the hero of the neoliberal narrative of universal competition."[21] This rationality is in many ways at odds with a democratic, political ethos – which is precisely why neoliberal societies need to hide and obscure their conflicting basis, for example by elevating meritocratic ideals. For contemporary democratic societies, as Thomas Piketty points out, "rest on a meritocratic worldview, or at any rate a meritocratic hope [. . .] a belief in a society in which inequality is based more on merit and effort than on kinship and inheritance."[22] However, as his own research has clearly documented, the main predictors of social positions are not effort or talent, but precisely kinship and inheritance.

In reality, then, the collective conviction that higher education is the path to income, status, and a good life may not only be a source of personal disappointment, but also, as Michael Sandel emphasises, a belief that actually *reinforces growing inequalities* in income and wealth. His reasoning is as follows: Meritocracy – a social system based on the belief that access to higher positions in society is a result of aptitude and achievements in the educational system – has the effect of representing all kinds of success, material and positional, as *being deserved*. In other words, the logic is that hard work and talent will be rewarded. Consequently, *if* it is true that the educational system is rigged for maximising opportunity based on merit, then when somebody does *not* succeed in this system it must be due to their lack of abilities, lack of effort, or both. This belief, Sandel argues, weakens resistance against growing inequality in status and income while the privileged elites, having attended the best universities, actually believe that they have earned their success.[23]

The (unfounded) belief in meritocracy, together with the increase of market mechanisms in the public sector, produces a toxic cocktail where both success and failure are seen as personal and due only to yourself. Such is the background, Sandel upholds, of all the prepping and personal investment in a college education that, when all is said and done, might still turn out to be of little value without the right personal *connections*. For in actuality, social mobility has *decreased* in the same period that meritocracy has become the norm in many countries, most markedly in the US, but increasingly in social democracies like Sweden. While inequalities in the Western world are on the rise, opportunities for social climbing through one's own effort and talent are diminishing. As Piketty notes, the strongest predictor of 'success' in work life, education and economy today is simply inherited wealth, making parental income "an almost perfect predictor of university access."[24] This brutal fact is effectively cloaked by the meritocratic narrative, where social inequalities are "legitimated as a failure of both aspiration and effort."[25] It is therefore no accident, according to policy researchers Robertson and Nestore, that "the rhetoric of 'rising' was at its most fulsome" in the US at a time when "inequality was approaching daunting proportions, with the richest 1%, taking more than the combined earnings of the entire bottom half [of] the population."[26]

An OECD report from 2018 titled "A Broken Social Elevator"[27] documents how opportunities for social mobility and improvement of life chances follow the parents' level of income, wealth and education – not only through one, but several generations. Important factors for social improvement and 'well-being,' according to the report, are education, access to health services, a taxation system and insurance against damage. Countries that have invested strongly in education in the past, such as the Nordic nations, offer more opportunities for social mobility: here the number of generations it would take for a person born into a low-income family (the bottom 10% of the income distribution) to reach the average in their societies is only 2 generations for Denmark and 3 for Finland, Norway and Sweden. The OECD average is 4.5 – but at the other end of the scale, where Brazil, China and South Africa can be found, it takes around 10 generations to advance to the average income. The report also shows that "children whose parents did not complete secondary school have only a 15% chance of making it to university compared to a 60% chance for their peers with at least one parent who achieved tertiary-level education."[28] This *educational disadvantage* follows people all their lives, the report states, creating a "vicious confluence" of low skills, limited employment prospects, exposure to environmental hazards and violence and shorter life expectancy.

In the US, where the gospel of meritocracy has been cultured from early childhood via Hollywood films, TV series and literature, the prospects for disappointment seem especially high. For without the right connections, the chances of success are slight and decreasing; hence the importance of being accepted at the 'right' university where, according to Sandel (a Harvard professor himself), the most important activity is networking. Access to relevant networks, the OECD also confirms, represents opportunities for the kind of 'well-being' that depends on socioeconomic status. Accordingly, Sandel drily notes, the rise of a "comping culture" illustrates how US college education has been transformed into "basic training for a competitive meritocracy, an education into packaging oneself and applying for stuff."[29]

The failed promise of meritocracy has serious socio-political consequences and leads to at least two kinds of discontent, as noted by Robertson and Nestore:

> One [discontent] is frustration that the system falls short of its meritocratic promise, especially if those who have worked hard and played by the rules (and invest a lot) are unable to advance. The other is the despair that arises when people believe the meritocratic promise has already been fulfilled, and they have lost out in the process. This is a demoralising discontent because it implies that for those who have been left behind their failure is their fault.[30]

Disappointment, discontent and receding empathy between classes tend to undermine the conditions for social solidarity and mutual recognition. But we also need to ask ourselves how education became a matter of competition – a 'squid game'[31] where the stakes and standards are constantly escalating. For there has been an on-going process, starting in the 1960s, whereby public education – which used to be organised according to national and local political processes – has been gradually reframed by a global economic system of benchmarking and standardised testing driven by organ-isations like the World Bank, the IMF, OECD and the EU.[32] This reframing is a central feature of the *human capital economics* that now dominates in large parts of the world. Based on the questionable premise of there being, as if by nature, a global competition between nations or regions, the leading idea is that knowledge and an educated and flexible population are forms of *capital* that can be mobilised in struggles for hegemony.[33]

At the individual level, the human-capital approach to education is ex-perienced through the discourse of 'responsibilisation' whereby politicians have shifted the burden of alleviating poverty from social arrangements into a personal responsibility to *improve oneself* more or less constantly. Individu-als, including children, are set to compete and fulfil a dream of success inside a scenario where anything but 'the best' is defined as 'failure.' Suing teach-ers and hiring personal coaches is part of the game, along with services that offer help for *academic* or *educational failure* – which is now recognised as a common cause for suicide in the most afflicted parts of the world.[34] Other products of this tyrannical race is plagiarism, essay mills, stand-ins for exams, bribery, cheating and family economies ruined by debt.

How did education become a matter of national competition? How did human beings become capital, and what encouraged individuals to compete on such terms? I believe that some of the forerunners (if not explanations) for the current situation can be traced to the period of the Cold War between the US and the USSR and their treatment of education and cultural policies. The remainder of this chapter will be devoted to this period and its afteref-fects: first, to explore the processes whereby education was transformed into an affair for the national economy, and then to take a look at the cultural battle over minds in Europe and the US. For although the regimes have changed, it seems to me that many conceptions formed during the Cold War concerning the political role of education are still with us to this day.

Sputnik and Beyond: Too Important for Educators

At various points in Western modernity, as Hannah Arendt is quoted in the opening of this chapter, education has been targeted as a starting point – a Point Zero – for amending society's deep, political concerns.[35] One of the most commented on examples in this respect is the American 'Sputnik cri-sis' of the late 1950s.[36] The triggering event was when the Soviet Union on 4 October 1957 unexpectedly launched the world's first artificial satellite, Sputnik 1, into orbit around the earth. The 'crisis' refers to the Americans' discovery that the Soviet Union was training two to three times as many scientists and engineers per year as the US.[37] So when the US and its allies suddenly realised that the USSR commanded technological capacities that not only challenged their position as the most advanced nations in the world but also potentially threatened the security of the North American continent, shockwaves were sent through the political apparatus and the public media. An 'education gap' was postulated, leading to massive investments in education at all levels, especially in basic science and technology. In 1961, when the OECD held its first conference about education, US Economic Counsellor Walter Heller famously stated that "in this context, the fight for education is too important to be left solely to the educators."[38] The Sputnik event drastically turned education in the US into a political issue, replacing the professional judgment of educators with political and technocratic expertise from sciences like economics and psychology.[39]

With Sputnik 1, a rhetorical chain of necessity was established between basic education, science and the military, forged around the fearful image of a rival superpower on the rise. For the Soviets had, according to the director of the US National Research Council's Office of Scientific Personnel, "subordinated their educational system to their overall policy of considering scientific and technical personnel as [a] most important factor in the total national military potential."[40] The Americans had to do the same: official reports were produced urging the United States and its allies to "immediately ratchet up the pace at which it produced its own scientific workers," since "American scientists and educators were losing key 'battles' in the 'cold war of the classrooms.'"[41] Accordingly, the Sputnik event led the US Congress to pass its first national law on education under the sinister title "The National Defense Education Act of 1958."[42] Worthy of note is that the Act came at a time when progressive, child-centred education was common practice in American classrooms, and so effectively heralded its end.

Echoes of American education draped in the rhetoric of war resound at later points in history, such as in the infamous report ordered by the Reagan administration, A Nation at Risk from 1983.[43] Here are the highly dramatic lines are from the opening statements:

> Our Nation is at risk. Our once unchallenged preeminence in commerce, industry, science, and technological innovation is being overtaken by competitors throughout the world. This report is concerned with only one of the many causes and dimensions of the problem, but it is the one that undergirds American prosperity, security, and civility. [. . .]
>
> If an unfriendly foreign power had attempted to impose on America the mediocre educational performance that exists today, we might well have

viewed it as an act of war. As it stands, we have allowed this to happen to ourselves. We have even squandered the gains in student achievement made in the wake of the Sputnik challenge. Moreover, we have dismantled essential support systems which helped make those gains possible. We have, in effect, been committing an act of unthinking, unilateral educational disarmament.[44]

The National Defense Education Act and *A Nation at Risk*, both produced during the Cold War, are among the most blatant examples of how questions about public education (in the US) have been framed as a geopolitical battle between regions and states. Inside this framework, education (education, education) is seen as necessary for the US's position in the world economy and arguably geopolitical hegemony.

Although the objectives are very different, there is an underlying *instrumentalism* toward education at play here that can also be recognised in the United Nations' framing of education as the solution to social ills such as poverty and injustices, referred to above, and also when the OECD posits education as the means for economic growth and social levelling. A common denominator for these phenomena is what educational historian Daniel Tröhler has called "educationalization": the tendency to frame various socio-political problems as "the result of deficits in the education system."[45] A much more direct expression for the same rhetorical move is used by educationist Joel Spring, namely, that politicians are likely to *blame schools*.[46] Spring asks: "Why do politicians primarily talk about crises in public education and offering educational solutions to problems not directly related to education such as poverty, national defense and global economic competition?" His answer is simple:

> Blaming schools makes good politics because otherwise politicians might have to blame corporate managers, factory owners for moving their factories off-shore, and leaders of financial institutions for economic problems. These are powerful and wealthy interests that can use their influence to thwart political ambitions. It is politically safe to just blame the schools.[47]

And true enough, since the Sputnik crisis – and notably in *A Nation at Risk* – American schools have regularly been blamed for the US lagging in global competition – even though, as Spring observes, scientists during the Sputnik era had actually been educated at a much earlier point, in the 1920s and 1930s, with no relevance for the state of American schools in the 1950s, child-centred or not.

Irrespective of this, the perception of an educational crisis led to a hectic activity to transform education into a 'first line of defense' by introducing new professionals such as economists, engineers and behavioural and cognitive psychologists into its field. These professionals developed instructional programmes based on behavioural and social-psychological principles accompanied by an advanced apparatus for testing individual abilities that was later to become a major industry. As summed up by Daniel Tröhler, "Teaching of school subjects should become efficient and individual; the catchword was 'programmed instruction,' and its central instrument was the teaching machine."[48] The teaching machine, although short-lived, was an early example of an individualised, computable learning programme developed by former military psychologist Burrhus Fredrick Skinner. Best known for his behaviourist principle 'operant conditioning' and the 'Skinner box' developed for pigeons, the legacy of B. F. Skinner is extremely interesting. For Skinner also wrote books, including a techno-utopian novel called *Walden Two*, where he reveals that his interest in learning was not primarily for the sake of efficiency – following the behaviourist formula of input and output – he also had a vision for society as a whole where he used education and behaviour modification to create a new social type, like another Rousseau. A visit to this remarkable work offers additional insight into the educational fronts at the time.

Walden Two, published in 1948, is the story of an engineered utopia, curiously named after Henry D. Thoreau's *Walden, or Back to the Woods* from 1854. 'Curiously' because Skinner's ideal community is a rather different version of the simple, self-sufficient life upheld by Thoreau. *Walden Two* is a fictive, ecological community organised according to rationalist principles using evidence-based methods for behaviour modification (Skinner's *experimentalism*). The ideals of *Walden Two* are communality, non-competitiveness and rationalism. None of its members work more than they have to, and every day they choose their own work tasks. Workload is weighted according to a rational time/interest ratio where the most boring or heavy work is assigned the fewest work hours – a principle securing that everything needed by the community gets done voluntarily and freely.

This extraordinary community is visited by the lead character, Burris,[49] who surprisedly observes how traditional, humanistic inclinations such as the esteem for free will and human dignity can be obstacles to more convincing (in the novel's universe) arguments about human nature and behaviour modification for the common good. Through behavioural engineering guided by experimentalist principles for social improvement, *Walden Two* trains young children to foster egalitarian and cooperative relationships. In the process, competitive sentiments are extinguished, along with unnecessary socially conditioned feelings like gratitude.

Walden Two spells out Skinner's deeper beliefs about how radical behaviour modification can be used for political purposes. For the fictive inhabitants of *Walden Two* have come to desire the things that are good for them, for the right reasons. His methods, however, were rather provocative at the time, and the characters of his novel also struggle to overcome their traditional, humanistic prejudices, but are finally convinced.

As odd as they may seem, Skinner's ideals are much closer to realisation today than in his own time. Many behaviourist principles are in current use: for example, the teaching machine exists in the form of various learning programmes and apps, while moderate forms of behaviour modification such as 'nudging' are used by government policy programmes across the world.[50] Non-consensual forms of behaviour modification also take place on a grand scale through social media. But where *Walden Two* was a green, rationalist utopia aiming at the common good, the forces that shape human behaviour through these technologies are part of a much more sinister confluence of profit motifs, military purposes and ideological dominance.[51]

The 1960s in the US was a very busy period for educational-psychological testing. School psychologists, often with connections to the military, produced a range of test batteries and instruments that have multiplied to this day.[52] Their impact was noticeable in Europe, where technocratic, often psychometric, approaches to education and more quantitative methods in the social sciences migrated from the US. In countries whose academic influence had been largely from Germany, like the Nordic region, a new rationalism was established during the post-war era connected to educational *planning*. This rationalism, which fits hand in glove with the 'human capital' approach to education and the so-called knowledge economy, was instrumental in turning 'knowledge' into an important economic factor.[53] Central drivers in this transformation were the OECD and the World Bank, whose annual reports monitor factors of 'input and output' in educational systems and relate them to variations in economic development – and in that process, introduced new concepts for quantification such as *learning output* and *learning outcomes*, which will be discussed in a later section.

The Cultural Cold War: Shaping of Mindsets

Shortly after the end of World War II, in which the US and USSR had been allies, they started to divide the world between them. Avoiding direct confrontation, both superpowers sought instead to extend their spheres of influence, politically and culturally. Confronted with internal opponents and fearing fifth-columnists on both sides, control over education, the media, art and culture were seen as no less important than arms. The USSR, for example, ran a broad university education aid program, launched by First Secretary Nikita Khrushchev in 1956, where foreign students were enrolled in Soviet universities across the region. Through this kind of 'soft power,' the Soviet Union could muster support for its own interests and foreign policy. Its long-term goals "typically centered on preparing the conditions, via the education of professionals as the future elites of home countries, for extended bilateral economic and trade relations" with the USSR, especially in countries emerging from colonial rule such as African nations.[54]

One of the more peculiar adventures during this period was the Congress of Cultural Freedom (CCF), founded in 1950 and covertly funded by the CIA.[55] The CCF was an influential, international association that recruited elite cultural and political intellectuals from the US and Europe. Its twofold aim was to "combat communist ideology" and to secure intellectual support for the Marshall Plan "in the sphere of culture and ideas."[56] Targeting anti-NATO intellectuals in Europe, the CIA was particularly interested in the Democratic Left and ex-leftists, and its conferences were attended by respected intellectuals such as Raymond Aron, Isaiah Berlin, Daniel Bell and Hannah Arendt. The CCF sponsored periodicals in various languages, expensive conferences and cultural festivals, and they promoted *abstract art* as opposed to art with a social content. Art is also where it made a lasting influence, according to James Petras:

> The CIA and its cultural organizations were able to profoundly shape the postwar view of art. Many prestigious writers, poets, artists, and musicians proclaimed their independence from politics and declared their belief in art for art's sake. The dogma of the free artist or intellectual, as someone disconnected from political engagement, gained ascendancy and is pervasive to this day.[57]

The aim of the CCF was thus to build adherence to the West by depoliticising intellectual and artistic work and thus weaken their capacity for bringing about political critique and social change.

Pockets of Resistance and Play

Under most regimes of dominance, there are also opportunities for alternative sub-regimes to emerge. The Cold War, in the East and West, was no exception. One interesting detail from US history is how many intellectuals on the American left, deprived of employment and publication opportunities by McCarthyist policies, found a political niche in children's literature. While mainstream American literature for young readers often bluntly reproduced social hierarchies and racial stereotypes, the League of American Writers (founded in 1935 by the Communist Party USA) saw children's literature as a suitable outlet for 'social messages' and an arena where intellectuals, especially women, could exert social and cultural influence while passing unnoticed.[58] Their books were picked up by another group of public-minded women, namely those working in libraries and bookshops.

In American classrooms, the Cold War was closing in on the curriculum until around 1950 when, historian Julia Mickenberg observes, history in textbooks had been "subordinated" to the struggle against Communism, and history was reduced to comparison of "the Russian and the American ways of life." In this process, "all references to poverty in America was eliminated, and the emphasis was on the United States' global leadership in 'the struggle for democracy.'"[59] But nonetheless, as long as teachers were able to organise their classes around problem-based learning – in line with the progressive education from the inter-war period – textbooks could be supplemented with alternative literature. Indeed, Mickenberg observes, the Cold War had created a market for these books:

> A significant proportion of trade children's books about American history and tradition, which escaped the kind of scrutiny paid to textbooks, represented a kind of return of the repressed. While civic education programs and history courses used textbooks glorifying America's heritage, supplementing these textbooks were dozens of Left-authored trade books on American history and folklore that drew upon American tradition in a very different way.[60]

Even at the height of the Cold War, when control of the workplace was at its tightest, literature for children was largely overlooked. According to Mickenberg, "the political power of imagination and play" was not recognised as a sufficiently subversive force, and thus a vast literature was allowed to grow with alternative stories about American and Western history, introducing other protagonists and non-hegemonic tales.[61]

The 20th century, despite its political disasters, saw a blossoming of social movements and alternative, progressive, child-centred pedagogies. Following John Dewey's Laboratory school (started in Chicago in 1894), which inspired educators across the world, many alternative schools using experimental methods were established, such as the Central European activity schools (*Arbeitsschule*); in the UK Alexander S. Neill founded Summerhill School in 1921; Waldorf education was started by Rudolf Steiner in Germany in 1919; France had Céléstin Freinet and Italy had Maria Montessori. Even in the early years of the USSR, the 1920s, more open forms of education were practiced and later forcefully removed by Stalin. When students revolted, the Summer of Love (Berkeley 1967) and May '68 transformed Western culture, and one might say that the ground – people's minds – had been prepared by so many school librarians, educators and teachers whose anti-authoritarian and child-centred pedagogy had been doing its work in local schools, universities, literature and the arts. This progressive impulse has continued to exist in tension, and sometimes in ambiguous alliance, with other educational imaginaries in Western modernity.

When Humans Became Capital

After the Cold War had ended and "the long 1968" had passed, a new discursive framework of a *knowledge economy* started to form in the industrialised parts of the world. But the political tensions from the Cold War period have not been resolved: Today we are once again seeing a race for world dominance between superpowers and geopolitical regions – notably the US, Russia, China – but this time around with new players in the big tech corporations, some of which control larger resources than nations do. Current battles for hegemony are closely related to intelligent systems and weapons technologies, surveillance, and control over data and space.

For the moment, I will focus on how notions of public education have been transformed via processes based on soft power and governance from the late 1980s to today. During this period, institutions of higher education across the globe have increasingly been rigged to compete for students, funding, and prestige, calling for a much tighter grip on their resources and organisation. This tightening is exerted through the soft power of *governance*, including the introduction of new terminology and frames of reference like intellectual property, human capital, learning outcomes and educational accountability. 'Learning' and 'knowledge' have become equivalents for capital in a competing world market, and enabled economists like Joseph Stiglitz and Bruce Greenwald to write books with telling titles such as *Creating a Learning Society: A new approach to growth, development and social progress*.

The OECD, the European Union and other international bodies established to promote economic cooperation and globalisation have been central in converting national education policies through international benchmarking systems.[62] We now have a vast apparatus of international ranking, benchmarking, and systems for accountability such as the PISA rankings, the IEA, the European Bologna system and various UN indices where *instrumentalism* is the guiding principle. The European Commission, for example, is exemplary clear on the new, economic function of universities:

Universities are key players in Europe's future and for the successful transition to a knowledge-based economy and society. However, this crucial sector of the economy and of society needs in-depth restructuring and modernization if Europe is not to *lose out in the global competition* in education, research and innovation.[63]

A key notion in the knowledge economy is that knowledge is a kind of capital. There are two different ways to conceptualise this notion, according to Mark Olssen and Michael Peters.[64] The first is that knowledge is embodied by individuals, where workers, technicians, scientists and entrepreneurs represent a form of capital that can be managed, invested in and at least partly managed through incentives. This capital is more or less flexible, using incentives to increase individuals' *mobility*. The second dimension of knowledge as capital occurs when knowledge is locked into structures such as firms. This capital is *not* very flexible. When Joseph Stiglitz and others state that knowledge, unlike other forms of capital, is not scarce but is more like a global public good – assumed to give increasing rather than decreasing returns on investments – they are mostly referring to knowledge that is openly shared. But knowledge-capital that is locked into structures through patenting, specialised technology, and so on, is not easily diffused, and does not increase with mobility.[65]

Also, as history shows, capitalism does not encourage openness but tends, instead, toward concentration of power, *including* the power of information and knowledge. The hailed knowledge society can thus be seen as yet another turn of the big wheel of capitalist accumulation, not least with today's giga-corporations such as Google (Alphabet), Microsoft, Facebook (Meta) and Amazon. To these corporations, people's *attention*, not their knowledge, is the main form of capital locked inside increasingly smarter systems. Indeed, as knowledgeable workers are replaced by artificial intelligence, the notion of 'a knowledge economy' may confer the false impression that subjects possessing knowledge are valuable, even dignified. But the knowledge that represents power today belongs to systems. In other words, as Shoshana Zuboff contends in her meticulous mapping of tech giants like Google, the knowledge economy was only a springboard to what she has called "surveillance capitalism."[66]

Return of the Teaching Machine

In retrospect it might be argued that the knowledge economy and human capital theory was always (or mostly) about opening new markets in the public sector. Public education in the US, for example – with scripted lessons accompanied by testing at every point of entry, promotion and movement between levels – has become a very lucrative market for tech vendors and corporations.[67] This rapidly spreading marketisation is accompanied by a de-professionalisation of teachers and devaluation of educational theory (the topic of chapter 3).

Artificial intelligence (AI) is especially attractive for educational contractors pushing into public school systems with technologies and tools for feedback, correction and assessment, learning programmes and personal guidance that largely reduce the need for a teacher. The main purpose of these technologies, according to educational policy researcher Kenneth Saltman, is to collect and manufacture data that produce capital for investors.[68] But tailored learning programmes based on AI – so-called *adaptive learning* – do not only have the side effect of making teachers redundant, he argues, they also represent a new, personally adapted version of the teaching machine that effectively squeezes out pedagogies based on questioning and dialogue. Adaptive learning technologies, Saltman observes, follow a logic of "techno-tracking" that makes a "longitudinal case out of the student."[69] One of the many problems with these technologies is that students' and teachers' subjectivities are delinked from their local and social context, with serious consequences for the opportunities for reflexive subject formation.

The learning theories that drive AI technology are positivist, focusing on behaviourist social-emotional learning and grit pedagogies.[70] These AI schemes, according to Saltman, "stand to completely displace the humanistic, social and democratic potential of public education in favour of making students into captured data engines, while those students are put on rigid tracks for the future by the very information they are compelled to produce."[71] It should come as no surprise that large, for-profit corporations have different goals than those that have been guiding public, democratic education. Nonetheless, the introduction of contemporary learning technologies represent a watershed, where "ownership, design and control of curriculum and pedagogical practice" is shifting from teachers to business, according to Saltman. Commenting on the larger picture, he continues:

> Bolstering a neo-liberal ideology that positions public education as business and in the service of business, ideologies of techno-utopian progress, techno-logical disruptions and the equation of technology with economic growth have played a large part in the rapid and exponential growth of digital technology in schools.[72]

The objective for these corporations, then, is not to develop self-disciplined, knowledgeable workers (in line with the knowledge economy), and even less to foster inquisitive, autonomous subjects, but instead to directly produce profit from students' bodies and behaviour.[73] With this rather sinister return of the teaching machine – but without Skinner's naïve belief in the good of behaviour modification – we are witnessing the perverted triumph of the Cold War doctrine that education is too important for educators.

I want to end this section with a few general reflections. Also looking back at the Cold War period from a European viewpoint, educational researchers Topolovčan and Dubovicki have identified what they see as a conflict between two different systems or approaches to education: One is a *technocratic* approach focusing on the notion of *curriculum* developed in the Anglo-American sphere (which they call an Anglo-Saxon concept and system). The other is the *humanistic* orientation of *pädagogik*, *didaktik* and *bildung* (these concepts were mentioned in the introduction; but see chapter 3 for a thorough discussion).[74] In the Anglo-Saxon system, the authors argue, education is conceptualised mainly through the logic of means and ends, informed primarily by psychology and principles of cost-effectiveness. This approach is for them an "implementation of practical needs arising from the Cold War" that stand in conflict with the historical European (mostly German) concept of education. Notably, the authors observe, the "Anglo-Saxon, Cold War concept of curriculum lacks a humanistic approach towards education"; an absence that represent an "enormous defect in modern education and the conceptualisation of future curricula."[75]

Of course, I do not mean to say (and probably nor do these authors) that American or British education *as such* are lacking a humanistic content. Rather, it is the policy approaches and organisation of the educational *systems* that are so ideologically different. Ian Westbury, Stefan Hoppman and Kurt Riquarts have similarly described an Anglo-American "curriculum tradition" that emphasises teaching methods, but with weak traditions for professionalism and teacher autonomy.[76] One might speculate whether this curriculum tradition is more vulnerable to assaults like school-blaming on the one hand and the pressure for responsibilisation of individuals (teachers and students) on the other. It would be too big a step, though, to claim that the on-going neoliberal and corporate transformations of the educational sector come as a result of the replacement of Continental with Anglo-American educational systems and traditions; but it is possible to observe a weakened resistance in the sector itself, which could very well be connected to a narrowing of perspective and a change of academic vocabulary. At least, it seems fair to assume that the introduction of practices aimed at increasing efficiency in learning (informed by psychology and economics) *at the cost of political and cultural orientation* risk making us lose sight of some historically very important aspects of educational theory, and consequently, diminished opportunities regarding professional self-understanding (for teachers) and resources for subject formation (for the student). The next two chapters will explore these ideas in more detail.

Notes

1. Aristotle, *The Politics*, book VIII, i. 1337a11 (London: Penguin, 1981).

2. Indeed, the potential to shape minds and behaviour through personalised electronic devices and the economic magnitude of the behaviour modification industry are of such scale that the traditional efforts of educators pale in comparison. Big tech also sees an enormous market in schools, in apps that collect user data to produce personalised tools for feedback, correction and assessment, and to sell for profit.

3. John Dewey, *Democracy and Education* (New York: Simon & Schuster, [1916] 1997), 87.

4. UDHR, https://www.un.org/en/about-us/universal-declaration-of-human-rights

5. The Norwegian Agency for Development Cooperation (NORAD), "Right to Education," accessed 13 August 2022, https://www.norad.no/en/front/thematic-areas/education/right-to-education/

6. UDHR, https://www.un.org/en/about-us/universal-declaration-of-human-rights

7. A translated excerpt of Abdul Rahman's letter was published in the Norwegian newspaper *Klassekampen*, 21 August 2021. Passages from the original letter are reprinted here with the author's permission.

8. Boko Haram is often translated as "Western education is forbidden," although Western 'civilization' might be a better translation, according to a declaration cited in "Boko Haram Resurrects, Declares Total Jihad," *Vanguard*, 14 August 2009, https://www.vanguardngr.com/2009/08/boko-haram-ressurects-declares-total-jihad/

9. UNESCO, "The Right to Education," accessed 3 August 2022, https://en.unesco.org/themes/right-to-education

10. NORAD, "Right to Education."

11. Not to mention the massive sexual abuse that has taken place in so many of these institutions.

12. C. A. Bowers, *The Culture of Denial. Why the Environmental Movement Needs a Strategy for Reforming Universities and Public Schools* (New York: SUNY Press, 1997).

13. "English as Medium of Instruction," accessed 3 August 2022, http://www.education.ox.ac.uk/our-research/research-groups/language-cognition-development/emi/

14. NORAD, "Right to Education."

15. See, e.g., Birgit Brock-Utne, "Language of Instruction and Student Performance," *International Review of Education* 53, no. 5/6 (2007).

16. The examples used here are those I have some experience with. They are not chosen as the most representative in any respect.

17. Rosemary Deem et al., "Transforming Higher Education in Whose Image?," *Higher Education Policy* 21, no. 1 (2008): 93.

18. Thomas Piketty, *Capital in the Twenty-First Century* (London: Belknap/Harvard University Press, 2014), 484.

19. Hartmut Rosa, *Alienation and Acceleration: Towards a Critical Theory of Late-Modern Temporality*, vol. 3., NSU Summertalk (Malmö: NSU Press, 2010).

20. Filiz Yaylaci, "Analysis of Suicides Related with Educational Failure," *The Anthropologist* 19, no. 2 (2015).

21. Niklas Angebauer, "Property and Capital in the Person: Lockean and Neoliberal Self-ownership," *Constellations* 27, no. 1 (2020): 51.

22. Piketty, *Capital in the Twenty-First Century*, 422.

23. Sandel, *The Tyranny of Merit*, 197ff.

24. Piketty, *Capital in the Twenty-First Century*, 485.

25. Susan L. Robertson and Matias Nestore, "Education Cleavages, or Market Society and the Rise of Authoritarian Populism?" *Globalisation, Societies and Education* 20, no. 2 (2022): 9.

26. Robertson and Nestore, "Educational Cleavages," 9.

27. The OECD report, "A Broken Social Elevator? How to Promote Social Mobility," OECD Publishing, Paris, 2018, https://doi.org/10.1787/9789264301085-en, is part of the Inclusive Growth Initiative.

28. OECD, "A Broken Social Elevator," 5.

29. Sandel, *The Tyranny of Merit*, 182.

30. Robertson and Nestore, "Educational Cleavages," 9.

31. "Squid game" is a massively popular network series from 2021, named after a Korean child's game. In the series' version of the game, players are lured into competing for a high money prize with their own lives as stakes. The series universe is one of exploitation, where gestures of solidarity and friendship are punished by the brutal game, thus illustrating the consequences of false hopes for upward mobility.

32. Deem et al., "Transforming Higher Education in Whose Image?"

33. Applauding and intensifying the human capital approach to education is a large industry that produces tests and test preparation material for use in public schools, simultaneously lobbying for English as a medium of instruction in order to expand globally. A thorough documentation of policy networks, acts, etc., can be found in Joel Spring, *The Politics of American Education* (New York/London: Routledge, 2011).

34. See, e.g., Sandel, *The Tyranny of Merit*, 180. An internet search of terms like 'education (or school) + ruin + life' will document the magnitude of the tragedy.

35. "The role played by education in all political utopias from ancient times onward shows how natural it seems to start a new world with those who are by birth and nature new." Hannah Arendt, *The Origins of Totalitarianism* (New York: Schocken, 2004), 173.

36. Hannah Arendt also refers to Sputnik, the satellite, in *The Human Condition* and to the Sputnik "shock" in "The Crisis in Education," both published in 1958.

37. These numbers were reproduced by the press without necessary qualifications, e.g., that the numbers of Soviet students of science and engineering included correspondence and extension students. See David Kaiser, "The Physics of Spin: Sputnik Politics and American Physicists in the 1950s," *Social Research* 73, no. 4 (2006): 1225–52.

38. Daniel Tröhler, "The Technocratic Momentum after 1945, the Development of Teaching Machines, and Sobering Results," *Journal of Educational Media, Memory, and Society* 5, no. 2 (2013): 1–19.

39. Tomislav Topolovčan and Snjezana Dubovicki, "The Heritage of the Cold War in Contemporary Curricula and Educational Reforms," *CEPS Journal* 9, no. 2 (2019): 18.

40. Kaiser, "The Physics of Spin," 1227.

41. Kaiser, "The Physics of Spin," 1227.

42. In fact, this education bill for federal funding of higher education was successfully renamed as a "defense act" to be able to pass Congress. See United States Senate, 4 October 1957, "Sputnik Spurs Passage of the National Defense Education Act," https://www.senate.gov/artandhistory/history/minute/Sputnik_Spurs_Passage_of_National_Defense_Education_Act.htm#:~:text=The%20National%20Defense%20Education%20Act%20of%201958%20became%20one%20of,and%20private%20colleges%20and%20universities

43. https://en.wikipedia.org/wiki/A_Nation_at_Risk

44. *A Nation at Risk*, https://www2.ed.gov/pubs/NatAtRisk/risk.html or https://web.archive.org/web/20201030104244/https://www2.ed.gov/pubs/NatAtRisk/risk.html

45. Tröhler, "The Technocratic Momentum," 1–2.

46. Spring, *The Politics of American Education*.

47. Spring, *The Politics of American Education*, 18.

48. Tröhler, "The Technocratic Momentum," 4.

49. The protagonist is a psychology professor named Burris: a name strongly suggestive of an alter ego. Burris has a friend named Castle, who teaches philosophy and ethics at the university. Castle engages in long conversations with Frazier, the founder of Walden Two. The initials of Burris and Frazier, as in B. F. Skinner, also hint to Skinner having a dialogue with himself; possibly struggling to rid himself of his own, non-rational humanism while simultaneously coming to terms with his tendencies to techno-rational hubris, embodied by Frazier.

50. See, e.g., Mark Whitehead et al., "Nudging All over the World: Assessing the Impacts of the Behavioural Sciences on Public Policy," ESRC Negotiating Neuroliberalism Project Report, 2014. Retrieved from https://changingbehaviours.files.wordpress.com/2014/09/nudgedesignfinal.pdf

51. Shoshana Zuboff, *The Age of Surveillance Capitalism* (London: Profile Books PublicAffairs, 2019).

52. In the US, the No Child Left Behind Act of 2001 was instrumental in launching the current global industry of educational testing, according to Spring, *The Politics of American Education*.

53. Spring, *The Politics of American Education*.

54. Tom G. Griffiths and Euridice Charon Cardona, "Education for a Social Transformation: Soviet University Education Aid in the Cold War Capitalist World-System." *European Education* 47, no. 3 (2015): 227.

55. Information about the CIA's funding of CCF was revealed to the general public in 1967, in connection with the Vietnam War.

56. Elena Aronova, "The Congress for Cultural Freedom, Minerva, and the Quest for Instituting 'Science Studies' in the Age of Cold War," *Minerva* (London) 50, no. 3 (2012): 308.

57. James Petras, "The CIA and the Cultural Cold War Revisited," *Monthly Review* 51, no. 6, November 1999, https://monthlyreview.org/1999/11/01/the-cia-and-the-cultural-cold-war-revisited/

58. Julia Mickenberg, *Learning from the Left: Children's Literature, the Cold War, and Radical Politics in the United States* (Oxford: Oxford University Press, 2006), 10, 13.

59. Mickenberg, *Learning from the Left*, 234.

60. Mickenberg, *Learning from the Left*, 235.

61. Mickenberg, *Learning from the Left*, 27.

62. See, e.g., the OECD's report series Education at a Glance, www.oecd.org/education/education-at-a-glance/

63. European Commission, 2006, emphasis added.

64. Mark Olssen and Michael A. Peters, "Neoliberalism, Higher Education and the Knowledge Economy: From the Free Market to Knowledge Capitalism," *Journal of Education Policy* 20, no. 3 (2005).

65. Olssen and Peters, "Neoliberalism, Higher Education and the Knowledge Economy."

66. Zuboff, *The Age of Surveillance Capitalism.*

67. Spring, *The Politics of American Education.*

68. Saltman, "Artificial Intelligence and the Technological Turn."

69. Saltman, "Artificial Intelligence and the Technological Turn," 202.

70. Grit pedagogy is often defined as perseverance combined with passion for a long-term goal and applies especially to character formation and academic achievement.

71. Saltman, "Artificial Intelligence and the Technological Turn," 202.

72. Saltman, "Artificial Intelligence and the Technological Turn," 198.

73. Saltman, "Artificial Intelligence and the Technological Turn."

74. Topolovčan and Dubovicki, "The Heritage of the Cold War." See also Ian Westbury et al., *Teaching as a Reflective Practice: The German Didaktik Tradition* (Mahwah, NJ: Lawrence Erlbaum, 2012).

75. Topolovčan and Dubovicki, "The Heritage of the Cold War," 13–14.

76. Westbury et al., *Teaching as a Reflective Practice: The German Didaktik Tradition* (Mahwah, NJ: Lawrence Erlbaum Associates, 2012).

CHAPTER TWO

~

Educational Imaginaries

From Investment to Question

So much hope is invested in the promise of education; but as we know, education does not always lead to the intended results. In the previous chapter we saw examples of how education – in practice and in theory – can be both a source of hope and of great disappointment. Sometimes 'education' can even take the form of abuse, where young children become their parents' or nation's 'investments' in the competition for prestige, power or 'success.' But this is only *one* conception, and a narrow one, of what the term 'education' can mean. In fact, it seems to me that some of the deeper tensions of modern societies are embodied in its various meanings. This chapter starts to explore these tensions more theoretically, looking especially at some of the concepts and ideas from Cornelius Castoriadis that were mentioned in the introduction. We begin with a common complication.

One of the possible 'side-effects' of education – especially at the higher levels – is that a student may, through the course of education, choose to develop along a different path than what was intended from the beginning. For example, students may become unruly and insubordinate and start to think for themselves in unwanted ways – sometimes to the point where they break with their teachers, family values, religious traditions and authorities. This is why students, as every totalitarian leader knows, are the first group they need to keep under control during a political conflict – and a reason for the enduring tensions between liberal forms of education and more reactionary imaginaries and belief systems. To be sure, every educational practice that encourages deeper kinds of questions, asking for reasons, evidence and justifications, immediately leads into problems when seen from the view-point of dogmatic religion. It would be too easy, however, to claim that the tendency toward closure and resistance against questioning is reserved for the most religious societies – rather, it is characteristic of all societies that value only *one* course of development, be it competition, economic growth, prestige, national glory or something else. In fact, no regime or society is en-tirely immune to the desire to close itself off against questions that threaten its own self-understanding. For example, one of the central tensions in mod-ern, Western societies concerns the coexistence of capitalist and democratic imaginaries, as two significations that may easily come into conflict. This conflict is an underlying premise for contemporary in various political theo-ries and notions of democratic citizenship (a more thorough discussion of citizenship theories will follow in chapter 4). Where some theories acknowl-edge these tensions, and question their compatibility, others are less reflex-ive, sometimes to the point where they endorse and uphold the status quo.

To monitor progress in civic and citizenship education, there are cross-national, comparative surveys monitoring young citizens' knowledge, at-titudes, and engagement for democracy, such as the Civic and Citizenship Education Studies (ICCS) organised by the International Association for the Evaluation of Educational Achievement (IEA).[1] In the ICCS studies, "civic knowledge about the existing political system" and "trust in national institu-tions" are found to correlate positively with "democratic ideals" such as toler-ance toward diversity, endorsement of immigrants' rights, and transnational cooperation.[2] These factors are considered as positive and worth cultivating in schools. However, due to the neoliberal framing of these studies – where "democratic ideals" very often refers to the facilitation of transnational mo-bility, especially in the European module of the survey – they fail to pick up on political movements that fall outside of their own categories of 'democ-racy,' such as politically subversive movements, and they have also failed, as noted by participating researchers, to detect the rise of nationalist populism in Europe.[3]

The European Union, for example, being both a set of principles for eco-nomic liberalisation and trade in a competing, global market economy and a project for European peace and stability, aims simultaneously at strengthen-ing Europe politically and economically while also endorsing cooperation in a range of areas. When citizenship is defined along both these dimensions at the same time, there is a tendency to favour the more technocratic, global-ist, EU-market-friendly definitions. A Danish study, for instance, shows how civic and citizen education in Denmark – like all the Nordic countries – has been driven in an increasingly "academic" direction focusing on civic knowledge and "functions" at the cost of the holistic, cultural approach known in Nordic schools.[4] Following OECD reforms for managing and increasing "effectiveness, accountability, benchmarks and national school monitoring systems" to its member nations based on models from New Zealand, Canada, the US and England, Danish citizenship education now finds itself in a tension between conflicting imaginary significations: on the one hand with a system rigged for effectiveness and academic outcomes and on the other a cultural ethos based in a humanistic-progressive tradition of "democratic bildung." The "advocates of the neo-liberal competitive state," as educational researcher Jens Brun calls them, see their opponents as "counterproductive and conservative (even nationalistic or populistic)" and failing to promote "an up-to-date and adequately globally competitive citizenry."[5]

The conflict between progressive (or post-progressive) and neoliberal conceptions pervades educational discourse, practice, policy and research in Denmark today, but there is a clear tendency, Brun argues, to reduce the importance of democratic education in favour of frameworks for educational effectiveness.[6] Similar tensions exist, for example, in educational systems that have constitutional commitments to *equality* on the one hand and on the other hand are drifting – or being pushed – toward global *competition for economic growth*.[7] These commitments are not necessarily in concordance, as we saw from the discussion about meritocracy in chapter 1. In her educational manifesto, *Not for Profit*, philosopher Martha Nussbaum identifies what has happened in nations that value economic growth *more* than democracy and human well-being, namely that:

> Curricular content has shifted away from [educational] material that focuses on enlivening imagination and training the critical faculties toward material that is directly relevant to test preparation. Along with the shift in content has come an even more baneful shift in pedagogy: away from teaching that seeks to promote questioning and individual responsibility toward force-feeding for good exam results.[8]

One of the effects of this shift is that the humanities are systematically defunded and marginalised, according to Nussbaum. "The student's freedom of mind is dangerous," she contends, "if what is wanted is a group of technically trained obedient workers to carry out the plans of elites who are aiming at foreign investment and technological development." Her reference here is government schools in the Indian province Gujarat where the curriculum, as she sees it, is designed to discourage critical thinking.[9]

While Nussbaum's examples are mostly from India and the US, the humanities have also lost ground in European universities. Across the globe – since Sputnik – universities competing in terms of technological innovation tend to favour and stimulate the STEM subjects (science, technology, engineering and mathematics). To be sure, these subjects are important to understand and engage with "wicked problems" such as climate change and techno-scientific developments, but nonetheless, as Nussbaum argues, subjects that nurture and value the imagination and empathy, such as literature and the humanities, are equally or even *more* needed in nations that want to be democratic – not least when societies need to change themselves.

Democracies, in the true sense of the term, *need* obstinate, critical citizens who are able to question common beliefs and instituted truth; their ideas and questions are the lifeblood that prevents democracies from turning into administrative and technocratic systems, oligarchies, autocracies or worse. In other words, democracies are not merely *systems* consisting of procedures, checks and balances that, once in place, can operate without any effort on the part of their members; they are political *regimes* where citizens effectively govern themselves. On this background we may recall Hannah Arendt's contention that "[t]he aim of totalitarian education has never been to instil convictions but to destroy the capacity to form any." To be sure, the true opponent of a regime that resists social change is the capacity of individuals and collectives to use their imagination creatively.

Cornelius Castoriadis: Education Is the Object of True Politics

The main theoretical source for the present study is the Greek-French philosopher and psychoanalyst Cornelius Castoriadis. In his groundbreaking work *The Imaginary Institution of Society* from 1975, Castoriadis develops a rich, conceptual apparatus that elucidates what a society is, how it is created, upheld and reproduced, and how societies change themselves historically and politically.[10] Castoriadis is also my resource for highlighting the 'doubleness' of certain concepts (most centrally, the notions of instituted and instituting society) and other forthcoming discussions. In the following, I will introduce some of Castoriadis's central concepts, not in any complete sense but enough to be able to use, apply and develop some of his central ideas.

The notion of the "imaginary institution" of society and its relevance for education in a political democracy represents a departure from more standard, contemporary political theory, most fundamentally because Castoriadis rejects the idea that there should be a difference in kind, a contradiction or opposition between *individuals* and *the social* which needs to be mediated.

His politico-educational thought is primarily concerned with fostering social and political creativity and democratic self-governance; but some of his ideas may at first glance seem to point in the opposite direction. One such notion is his conceptualisation of *the individual*. Being an individual, for Castoriadis, simply means to be part of the social, which makes 'the individual' a strictly sociological concept. Consequently, individuals cannot be socialised to anything 'else' than the historical society to which they belong. Different societies foster certain social types, as Aristotle said, and Plato before him: "The democratic spirit promotes democracy and the oligarchic spirit oligarchy," and so forth.[11] An aspect of this idea is that individuals' schooling is essential for maintaining and upholding a given social form or regime.

It would be an illusion – and a dangerous one, as we saw from the discussion about meritocracy – to think that individuals are free to become whatever they like. But that is exactly what the neoliberal credo implies. As Castoriadis points out, we can become many things, but only those kind of things that are instituted as meaningful in the societies of which we are a part. And likewise in education: no educator can succeed in bringing forth a social type from an entirely different historical epoch, however hard they try. In Castoriadis's words: "What is in question here [in 1975] is forming the individual as capitalist or proletarian, and not as lord, patrician or Amon-Râ priest." These are socially instituted types, and "[n]othing in the psyche as such can produce *these* significations, the *world* of significations without which they are nothing, the *mode of being* of these significations as instituted."[12] As he explains: "Our relation to the social – and to the historical which is its unfolding in time – cannot be called a relation of dependence, for this would be meaningless. It is rather a relation of *inherence*."[13] In short, significations are of the social, and so are individuals.

This point is repeated in no lesser terms in Castoriadis's later works. In a speech from 1981, "The Imaginary: Creation in the Social-Historical Domain," for example, he claims that "[w]e are all, in the first place, walking and complementary fragments of the institution of our society – its 'total parts,' as a mathematician would say. The institution produces, in conformity with its norms, individuals that by construction are not only able but bound to reproduce the institution."[14] Similarly, in "Democracy as Procedure and Democracy as a Regime" from 1997: "The individual *is* society, a fragment at the same time as a miniature – or, better, a sort of hologram – of the social world."[15]

As all these examples show, the socialisation of the individual is in a certain sense total for Castoriadis – but this is only one aspect of a larger picture, for the same is not true for the individual *psyche*. According to Castoriadis, "the psyche of each singular human being is not and can never be *completely* socialized and rendered exhaustively conformal to what institutions demand of it,"[16] partly because the instituted society is under constant pressure to change itself and partly because the nucleus of the psyche holds a surplus of undetermined meaning which Castoriadis calls the *radical imagination.*

By underscoring the overlap between individuals and their societies' instituted form, Castoriadis *could* be taken to mean that political resistance and questioning of established structures is impossible. But this is exactly the opposite of what he means and intends: instead, the conceptual clarification is directed against the rather naïve opposition between individuals on the one side and everything collective – "structures" – on the other. A totalising conception of the instituted society is not what Castoriadis is after; on the contrary, his point is to explain what it means to be individuated and what the social conditions for political creativity are.

To fully grasp this point, we also need to understand Castoriadis's notion of the social and its imaginary, self-creative dimension. For Castoriadis, the social – or better, a society as instituted form – consists of two instances: that which creates itself, "the instituting society" (*l'instituant*), and that which is created, "the instituted society" (*l'instituée*). "The self-institution of society," for Castoriadis,

> is the creation of a human world: of "things," "reality," language, norms, values, ways of life and death, objects for which we live and objects for which we die – and of course, first and foremost, the creation of the human individual in which the institution of society is massively embedded.[17]

As we can now begin to see, the imagination is both a mode of being for the psyche (the radical imagination) and a dimension of the social which Castoriadis calls "the instituting imaginary." It is the instituting imaginary that creates society – or rather, society creates itself through its instituting imaginary – and produces the *social imaginary significations* that permeate everything in it, infusing society with meaning, direction and orientation.[18] Social imaginary significations are not fixed entities, but rather the "emerged parts of the magma of social imaginary significations instituted each time by society and which hold society together."[19] They are "imaginary" in so far as they refer to a human world of significations; and the main way they are instituted is through the socialisation process where they are invested by the individual psyche as meaningful, providing direction and orientation for individuals' lives.

A society, Castoriadis tells us, creates itself as a meaningful form (Greek: *eidos*). However, there is always a surplus of imaginary meaning in the social, which is why he talks of the instituting as something *more* than the instituted form:

> There will always be a distance between society as instituting and what is, at every moment, instituted – and this distance is not something negative or deficient; it is one of the expressions of the creative nature of history, what prevents it from fixing itself once and for all into the "finally found form" of social relations and of human activities, what makes a society always contain *more* than what it presents.[20]

The potential for self-reflexiveness at the social level is found in the activation of this imaginary surplus. Accordingly, societies can institute themselves as more or less open to their own capacity for self-creation and change. In dichotomous terms, they can institute themselves as self-reflexive with institutional arrangements for critical self-questioning and efficient self-governance, as in a (real) democracy, or they can institute themselves as more or less closed forms whose meaning cannot be questioned by its members in any meaningful way. Of course, in principle every meaning can be questioned – but in social reality, if political and philosophical questioning is not experienced as meaningful by a society's members, it will not take place on any major scale.

There is an important difference here between explicitly authoritarian societies, where resistance is experienced as meaningful but dangerous, and those whose significations have been sealed off in more silent, indirect manners, such as the totalitarian kind of schooling aimed at destroying the very capacity to form independent convictions. I will return to these ideas in later sections, but for now, let us maintain the central implication that the potential and opportunities for political questioning, including the formation of an autonomous subjectivity, are *inherently social*. More precisely, they emerge in the perceived tension between the instituting and the instituted society and its specific imaginaries.

It is now time to become more concrete in terms of education, which for Castoriadis is a political matter par excellence. In his own words, "the object of true politics is to transform institutions, but to transform them in such a way that those institutions educate individuals, putting them on the road to autonomy."[21] How this can be done, is a paradox.

Freedom and the Paradox of Subjectivity

Education and politics belong – together with psychoanalysis – to the domain of praxis which Freud termed "the impossible professions."[22] They are "impossible" since they engage directly with relationships between people whose personal agendas vary, and therefore their results are beyond control. Politics, for example, deals with opinions about what kind of social arrangements are desirable, but it cannot escape the fundamentally human condition that people see the world from different viewpoints and therefore desire or need different and sometimes incompatible things. In education, educators may have an 'educational' agenda while the other person (student) is free to set their own goals: independently and increasingly with age. It is therefore impossible to educate somebody against their will – and neither education nor politics can be expected to unfold according to a detailed, preconcieved plan.

On a more principled level, there are no ahistorical, technical or transcendental objectives for mankind toward which these impossible professions can be directed without stirring up questions about the legitimacy or justification of aims and means. Indeed, the outcomes of politics, education (and psychoanalysis) depend less on a professional practitioner than on the person(s) or society in question. For this reason, it is impossible to separate the aims from means, activities and processes in these domains of action: the aim is inside, or emerges with, the process.

The impossible professions do not abide by the technical knowledge of *poeisis* (a process of making something), but by the practical wisdom of *praxis* (acting-doing) where there is no separation between ends and means. A good illustration, also used by Castoriadis, is the notion of subjectivity. When we talk about subjectivity as an aim for democratic education – a subjectivity that is also central in politics and psychoanalysis – it is a subjectivity that emerges with and through the educational process itself. Castoriadis describes subjectivity (here with reference to the psychoanalytic process) as follows:

> The emergence of a reflective and deliberate – that is to say, autonomous – subjectivity can be defined as the end of the analytic process [. . .]. We can consider this type of subjectivity as the formal norm of human beings. And we can also consider the activity of the genuine analyst – who aims at the emergence of the autonomy of the patient by "using" for this purpose the potential elements of this same autonomy – as a formal model for all human praxis. Such praxis may be defined as the activity of an autonomy that aims at the autonomy of one or several others – which is what genuine pedagogy and genuine politics also do or should do. Here we find the answer to the question: How is the action of one freedom upon another freedom possible?[23]

What Castoriadis addresses here is a version of the classical "paradox of education," first formulated by Immanuel Kant in "Über Pädagogik": How can we justify to interfere with the freedom of another person with the purpose of fostering their autonomy? In other words, we use means that interfere with another person's freedom before they are in the position – due to their young age or lack of knowledge – to endorse or sanction our interference.[24] This paradoxical idea related to freedom and autonomy has existed at least since Rousseau. It is well-known in the Northern European tradition of *pädagogik* and is contained in the German and Scandinavian notion of bildung.[25] But the interesting step made by Castoriadis is to transpose the paradox from psychoanalysis and education to politics and society, where it is made to define what he calls "genuine (or true) politics." In genuine politics and a certain kind of education – here called "genuine pedagogy" and in other texts, *paideia*[26] – the aim is a subject that is capable of setting its goals for itself, to reflect upon them, and take responsibility for their self-reflexive own self-formation.[27]

As I have already argued, the resources for this type of self-reflexive subjectivity are in and of the social: they can only thrive within specific social-historical forms, and vice versa. The imaginary significations that characterise these social-historical forms are upheld by the society's members. Hence the intimate connections between education and politics for Castoriadis.

In an interview from 1991, published under the title "Psyche and Education," Castoriadis laments that contemporary political philosophy has overlooked the question of education, "which was the main concern of all the great philosophers, starting with Plato and Aristotle and up to Rousseau." As already mentioned, for Castoriadis "[t]he object of true politics is to transform institutions, but to transform them in such a way that those institutions educate individuals, putting them on the road to autonomy."[28] In other words, when political theorists ignore the question of education, their theories will not be able to elucidate or contribute to the political project of autonomy, which for Castoriadis is the aim of true politics as it has been instituted at various points in history, for example, in the first democracy, in medieval Italian city states and in workers' councils and movements.

However, because every society tends toward closing off its horizon of meaning, autonomy or self-governance is not something that can be instituted once and for all. Rather, the socially instituted meaning of autonomy must be constantly maintained and invested with meaning. The autonomy project is therefore like a source of water that must be kept running through permanent processes of questioning. In this respect, education is as important as political institutions for Castoriadis.[29]

This completes the conceptual cycle and allows us to see that for Casto-riadis, human beings are not only the sociological category of *individuals*; they are also potentially self-reflexive *subjects* capable of social creativity. We could say that the subject, in Castoriadis's rendering, refers to an individual who has *realised* their individuality in a society where freedom and autonomy are instituted. The discussion about autonomy continues below. But first, I would like to elucidate the process of subject formation a bit further, and in so do-ing, to complement the discussion about subject formation and subjectivity with a few concepts from the theory of intersubjective recognition – ideas that Castoriadis himself did not consider to be central, but which I think are needed to flesh out a full theory about democratic-political education inside institutions.

Intersubjectivity: Linking Institutions and Subjectivity

The specific way that the institution of society is internalised in individuals and the way personal subjectivity is formed is not elaborated in any detail by Castoriadis.[30] However, in order to formulate a differentiated notion of (po-litical) socialisation, including democratic citizenship and political agency, additional theoretical reflections at the level of intersubjectivity are needed. Axel Honneth's Hegelian theory of intersubjective recognition offers a con-ceptual apparatus that fills this niche quite well.[31] Honneth's central thesis in *The Struggle for Recognition* is that important aspects of our subjectivity are formed through experiences with concrete others: experiences where recog-nition is either granted or denied.

First of all, the kind of recognition referred to here is not associated with fame or status. Instead, recognition theorists like Axel Honneth, G. W. F. Hegel, Nancy Fraser, Charles Taylor and others consider recognition to be a basic, social need and a central element of socialisation. The essential idea in this tradition is that concrete experiences with others in the form of con-ferred or withheld recognition (misrecognition) are constitutive for subject formation by giving rise to forms of self-perception and identities that can only be actualised intersubjectively.

Consider for example how it is possible to become someone who sees themself as a good person. How can we know, simply from ourselves, whether we are good or bad? Or an even better example, how can we come see our-selves as someone who is funny and humorous? Clearly, in order to form such self-conceptions, certain experiences with others are needed. In the case of being funny, we *need* the experience of evoking laughter, smiles and cheers in other people. Similarly, in order to see ourselves as good or bad, we observe how others – who are also subjects worthy of *our* respect – react to and treat us. According to the theory (or theories) of recognition, the reactions and expectations we are met with from (significant) others, and their recognition of us as somebody *worthy* of *their* respect, love and attention, fundamentally shape our conceptions of ourselves as unique persons with specific, respectable attributes.

In Honneth's rendering, there are three 'patterns of recognition' that take place in three corresponding 'spheres of interaction.' All three types of recognition are necessary in order to develop the kind of positive self-relation that amounts to what he calls *self-realisation*. The three spheres are 1) the family and close friendship, where personal and basic emotional needs are either recognised or denied, 2) the juridico-public sphere of moral responsibility, where we may have the experience of being respected as bearers of equal rights, and 3) the socio-public sphere of solidarity, where persons are recognised for their unique traits and abilities. To be recognised in this last respect represents the possibility for developing self-esteem, and for the fullest realisation of ourselves, when we experience that our contributions to a community are valued as unique by bringing something of value to the world that only *we* can bring. In higher education, for example, the identity of being a scholar develops through processes where a person is recognised for their unique contributions to an ongoing scholarly conversation. This third sphere is also the most interesting dimension for our discussion of what Honneth calls 'the social grammar of recognition.'

Overall, recognition can take place when other persons whom we count as worthy of our recognition recognise us as unique persons with specific needs, rights, qualities and capabilities that deserve respect. Through this mutual act of recognition and self-identification, a person's potential qualities are brought forth and allowed to flourish as realised or actualised skills and qualities. For, according to Honneth,

> although we make manifest, in our acts of recognition, only those evaluative qualities that are already present in the relevant individual, it is only as a result of our reactions that he [sic] comes to be in a position to be truly autonomous, because he is then able to identify with his capabilities.[32]

All the examples above refer to processes of 'successful' intersubjectivity, but of course, not all intersubjective relationships are of this kind, as recognition is often withheld and denied, sometimes with what Honneth has called 'pathological' effects for the person or the community in question. The point to keep, though, is that theories of recognition show in some detail how the resources for subject formation are of a social nature – this time focusing on concrete experiences rather than socially instituted meaning. When reading Honneth with Castoriadis, or vice versa, we can now see that even though individuals *are* "fragments" or "embodiments" of the social institutions (Castoriadis) the specific ways they are able to realise their individuality are unique and socially differentiated (Honneth). As Johann Arnason puts it, individuals are *selective* embodiments of the institutions,[33] and their capabilities are more or less allowed to flourish, dependent on their social position *and* their personal experiences.

Also interesting for our discussion is that the purpose of recognition for Honneth is *autonomy*. In his own words, "only the person who knows that she is recognized by others can relate to herself rationally in a way that can, in the full sense of the word, be called 'free.'"[34]

> For it is only due to the cumulative acquisition of basic self-confidence, of self-respect, and of self-esteem – provided, one after another, by those three forms of recognition – that a person can come to see himself or herself, unconditionally, as both an autonomous and an individuated being and to *identify with his or her goals and desires.*[35]

On this note, let us now turn to the concept of autonomy and take a closer look at some of its meanings in politics and education.

Autonomy in Politics and Education

Autonomy is a central concept with diverse meanings in Western philosophy. In the following, I introduce some of its common uses and then give a more specific account of its place in educational theory. This discussion will continue in later sections, then specifically oriented around Castoriadis's notion of autonomy as being simultaneously an individual and a collective project (chapter 3). But at this point, I will limit the discussion to some general (conceptual and historical) points.

The Greek roots of the term are *autos*: self, and *nomos*: custom or law. *Nomos* was posited in Greek philosophy as a contrast to *physis* (nature) to circumscribe the social world and matters that depend on us as human beings. One of the many possible translations of *autonomy* is *self-governance*: to follow laws given by oneself in contrast to being under laws imposed by others (heteronomy). The concept has both technical-descriptive uses (as in systems theory) and normative definitions related especially to freedom. In modern philosophy and educational theory, autonomy is mostly associated with individual morality or ethics, while in political theory the term has strong connotations to Western political liberalism.

Since Immanuel Kant, the notion of (individual) autonomy refers to being cognitively capable, free and courageous enough to make use of one's own reason (*Vernunft*), which for Kant means to willingly follow the moral laws that a subject imposes on itself.[36] The motto *Sapere aude* – dare to know – as set forth in Kant's pamphlet *What Is Enlightenment?* is both a programme for the age of Enlightenment and an ideal of personal freedom with strong appeals to self-education. The foundations for this modern notion of autonomy are the individual's capacity to make decisions based on reasons (as opposed to whims of nature, i.e., subordination), to reflect and deliberate over ends and to commit to a purpose – in short, we are looking here at a *reasoning* form of agency. Acting autonomously in this (dominant) philosophical tradition means to act from reasons that are (considered to be) one's own, that is, independent of *others'* reasons.[37] As I have already argued, to educate toward this end entails a paradox.

Being the Author of a Life

The formal, Kantian conception of autonomy is strongly present in educational theory, although rarely in a pure form. Most of the time autonomy has become entangled with other concepts such as authenticity, enlightenment and liberty or freedom. In Northern European *pädagogik*, for example, the concept of (individual) autonomy has become historically intertwined with the Romantic ideal of authenticity to form the idea of a naturally unique self in need of protection and careful cultivation. This notion of an unspoiled, authentic or natural personality is at the core of the child-centred, progressive education from the twentieth century, with resonance up to this day.

Autonomy as authenticity is in many ways a counter-ideal to modernity's technical-rational forms of civilisation. At the root of this conceptual entanglement we find, as in so much of educational thought, Jean-Jacques Rousseau and his educational novel *Emile ou de l'éducation*. When working out his politico-educational thought, Kant was intrigued by Rousseau's notion of freedom – "the liberty which is self-enacted law rather than mere willful resistance to arbitrary coercion"[38] – and used it to develop his own concept of transcendental freedom. Self-enacted or self-imposed law – the principle of self-binding – is for Kant a voluntary decision with civilising purposes. Likewise, Rousseau's reason for letting *nature* be the child's educator was not that he was against self-discipline; on the contrary, as educational philosopher Eamonn Callan observes,

> [t]he education of Émile was designed not merely to evoke a stable rational self that would rule against the grain of custom and social prejudice; it would also encompass our natural passions, most notably the compassion by virtue of which self-interestedness could be muted and reconciled to the interests of others.[39]

Forming a self that is authentic, good-natured and unsubdued by society's false and corrupted customs is the prime educational task for Rousseau. To this purpose, one of his principles is that children are entitled to learning to know the world through their own active engagement with it rather than *via* words of teaching or books. By engaging directly with nature – carefully laid out by his tutor as puzzles and tasks for Emile to solve – the natural child, Emile, would learn to practice self-control by experiencing and considering the consequences of his actions.[40] Paradoxically, however, the education of Emile was far from natural in the sense of non-interference; on the contrary, his tutor was highly manipulative in rigging Emile's environment to teach him various, pre-planned educational lessons.

Rousseau's idea of education as *problem-solving in an environment* was elaborated in more practical and realistic terms by John Dewey when he founded (together with Jane Addams) the Laboratory school. The central principle, for Rousseau and Dewey, is that education should not be formal and abstract, but that students should engage with real-life problems, that is, *authentic concerns.* The idea of the natural child, and childhood as a unique life-form which deserves to have its own protected space – a world reigned by imagination, pretend and play, which in itself is a serious business – reverberates in Swedish educator Ellen Key's *Century of the Child*, in Pestalozzi and in Fröbel's Kindergarten, in Maria Montessori's dictum that play is the work of the child, in Rudolf Steiner's Waldorf education, in American progressive education, in Summerhill, in the ideas of Célestine Freinet, in Sigmund Freud's theory of childhood sexuality and in the UN Convention of the Rights of the Child. Likewise, education in and by nature is a very strong ideal in Norwegian education, for example when children in many primary schools spend every Monday, all year round, walking around in a near-by forest, however small. Among the most stringent protectors of childhood is Hannah Arendt. When Arendt claims that children, like everything that grows, need to "grow in the dark," undisturbed by the needs and projections of adults, it is also an echo of *Emile*.[41]

In educational theory, then, the ideal of autonomy as authenticity is not so much related to independence as the idea of being the author of a life – and not merely subjected to it – and creating a life story that is *meaningful*. This notion also resonates with the German Neo-humanists, not least Wilhelm von Humboldt's conception of Bildung as an enrichment of the self through engagement with literature, music, art and a wide variety of experiences. As Humboldt famously stated:

> It is the ultimate task of our existence to achieve as much substance as possible for the concept of humanity in our person, both during the span of our life and beyond it, through the traces we leave by means of our vital activity. This can be fulfilled only by the linking of the self to the world to achieve the most general, most animated, and most unrestrained interplay.[42]

One of the most pressing questions for Rousseau is whether the formation of autonomous authenticity can take place independently from social setting, for example whether it can succeed in a society that does not value such a project. Rousseau's problem in *Emile* was exactly this: how – if at all – can good persons be educated in a society that is bad and corrupted? His solution, if it can be called one, was to create a protected environment for the boy Emile where every kind of social influence was eliminated except for his dedicated but invisible teacher. In other words, Rousseau did not believe that individuals can live in a society without being decisively shaped by its social imaginaries.

Of course, *Emile* was never an example to follow – but its historical importance can hardly be exaggerated. One of the main lessons we have from Rousseau is that political reflections, or more broadly, reflections about the instituted and instituting society are essential in the philosophy of education: even the most conservative thinkers today recognise that educators cannot take as their starting point just *any* kind of existing social practice but must choose what they see as most valuable or edifying, worthy of being called 'our tradition' or vision of a 'better' world. Rousseau also highlighted the political importance of education and opened up one of the many meanings of what education is and ought to be. This will be the theme of the next chapter.

Notes

1. CIVED 1999, ICCS 2009 and ICCS 2016. The IEA is also responsible for PISA, TIMSS, PIRLS and monitoring progress toward the Sustainable Development Goal no. 4: Obtaining Quality Education for All.

2. From the report: "The role of schools in developing students' civic knowledge perhaps assumes even greater importance given the associations between students' level of civic knowledge [. . .] and students' positive attitudes toward equal rights for immigrants and toward freedom of movement within Europe. [S]tudents with higher levels of civic knowledge tended to be the students expressing more tolerant attitudes. They were also more in favor than their less knowledgeable peers of cooperation among European countries." Losito et al., "Main Findings," in *Young People's Perceptions of Europe in a Time of Change: IEA International Civic and Citizenship Education Study 2016 European Report* (Cham: Springer Open, 2018).

3. Erik Amnå, "The Personal, the Professional, and the Political: An Intertwined Perspective on the IEA Civic Education Studies," in *Influences of the IEA Civic and Citizenship Education Studies: Practice, Policy, and Research Across Countries and Regions*, ed. Barbara Malak-Minkiewicz and Judith Torney-Purta (Cham: Springer, 2021).

4. Jens Brun, "Civic and Citizenship Education in Denmark 1999–2019: Discourses of Progressive and Productive Education," in *Influences of the IEA Civic and Citizenship Education Studies: Practice, Policy, and Research Across Countries and Regions*, ed. Barbara Malak-Minkiewicz and Judith Torney-Purta (Springer, 2021), 56.

5. Brun, "Civic and Citizenship Education in Denmark," 57.

6. Brun, "Civic and Citizenship Education in Denmark."

7. Martha C. Nussbaum, *Not for Profit: Why Democracy Needs the Humanities* (Princeton, NJ: Princeton University Press, 2010).

8. Nussbaum, *Not for Profit*, 134.

9. Nussbaum, *Not for Profit*, 134.

10. *The Imaginary Institution of Society* was translated into English in 1987 but was first released in 1975 as *L'Institution Imaginaire de la Société* (Paris: Seuil, 1975).

11. Plato, *The Republic*, book 8; Aristotle, *The Politics*, book VIII, i. 1337a11.

12. Cornelius Castoriadis, *The Imaginary Institution of Society*, trans. Kathleen Blamey (Cambridge, MA: MIT Press, 1987), 318.

13. Castoriadis, *The Imaginary Institution*, 112.

14. Cornelius Castoriadis, "The Imaginary: Creation in the Social-Historical Domain," in *World in Fragments: Writings on Politics, Society, Psychoanalysis, and the Imagination*, trans./ed. David Ames Curtis (Stanford: Stanford University Press, 1997), 7.

15. Cornelius Castoriadis, "Democracy as Procedure and Democracy as a Regime," *Constellations* 4, no. 1 (1997): 2.

16. Castoriadis, "Democracy as Procedure," 3.

17. Cornelius Castoriadis, "The Greek *Polis* and the Creation of Democracy," in *Philosophy, Politics, Autonomy: Essays in Political Philosophy*, ed. David Ames Curtis (New York/Oxford: Oxford University Press, 1991), 84.

18. In "The Social-Historical," Castoriadis writes that social imaginary significations "construct (organise articulate, vest with meaning) the world of the society

considered and determine at the same time the representations, the affects, and the intentions dominant in a society" (231). Although I prefer the more precise and well-defined term 'social imaginary significations,' I have also used the more widespread term 'social imaginaries' interchangeably.

19. Castoriadis, "Power, Politics, Autonomy," 144.

20. Castoriadis, *The Imaginary Institution*, 113–14.

21. Cornelius Castoriadis, "Psyche and Education," in *Figures of the Thinkable*, trans. Helen Arnold (Stanford, CA: Stanford University Press, 2007), 175.

22. *Die unmöglichen Berufe*, see Cornelius Castoriadis, "Psychoanalysis and Politics," in *World in Fragments*, ed./trans. David Ames Curtis (Stanford: Stanford University Press, 1997), 126ff.

23. Cornelius Castoriadis, "Psychoanalysis and Philosophy," in *The Castoriadis Reader*, ed./trans. David Ames Curtis (Oxford: Blackwell), 360.

24. Alexander von Oettingen, *Det pædagogiske paradoks: en grundstudie i almæn pædagogik* (Århus: Klim, 2001).

25. The terminology varies between countries: *Bildung* (German), *danning* or *dannelse* (Norwegian and Danish) and *bildning* (Swedish). In the following I shall use the term '*bildung*' with a lower case 'b.' For an elaboration, see Straume "Bildung from Paideia to the Modern Subject."

26. *Paideia* is the Greek equivalent of *bildung*. See chapter 4 for a discussion.

27. Castoriadis, "Psychoanalysis and Politics," 126 ff.

28. Castoriadis, "Psyche and Education," 175–76.

29. Castoriadis, "Power, Politics, Autonomy," 161–62.

30. Castoriadis also admitted that he would have liked to have spent more time on education in "Done and to Be Done," in *The Castoriadis Reader*, ed./trans David Ames Curtis, 361–417 (Oxford: Blackwell, 1997).

31. Axel Honneth, *The Struggle for Recognition: The Moral Grammar of Social Conflicts* (Cambridge: Polity, 1995). I have mainly used the Norwegian translation from the German, which means that some of my terms may diverge from the English translation.

32. Axel Honneth, "Grounding Recognition: A Rejoinder to Critical Questions," *Inquiry*, 45, no. 4 (2002): 510. Published as the afterword to the Norwegian translation of 2008.

33. Johann Pàll Arnason, personal correspondence.

34. Honneth, "Grounding Recognition," 509.

35. Honneth, *The Struggle for Recognition*, 169, emphasis added.

36. Kant's notion of autonomy refers to the will. See https://plato.stanford.edu/entries/kant-moral/#AutFor.

37. Formal and person-oriented notions of autonomy defined mainly as independence are fully compatible with neoliberal ideals of meritocratic competition and apolitical governance, especially when used without the Kantian implications of reason and moral law. There is, however, a risk that individual autonomy can turn into an almost antisocial concept. Making choices without consideration of what others think can simply be inconsideration, as both Rousseau and Kant were very aware of.

38. George Armstrong Kelly, "Rousseau, Kant, and History," *Journal of the History of Ideas* 29, no. 3 (1968): 347.

39. Eamon Callan, "Autonomy," in *Encyclopedia of Educational Theory and Philosophy*, ed. D. C. Phillips (Thousand Oaks, CA: SAGE, 2014), 71.

40. The free and natural education was reserved for boys. Sophie, Emile's intended wife, was under no such regime, but simply educated to please and be of use to Emile.

41. Hannah Arendt, "The Crisis in Education," in *Between Past and Future: Eight Exercises in Politic Thought* (New York: Penguin, 2006).

42. Wilhelm von Humboldt, "The Theory of Bildung," trans. Gillian Horton-Krüger, in *Teaching as a Reflective Practice: The German Didaktik Tradition*, ed. Ian Westbury et al., 57–61 (Mahwah, NJ: Lawrence Erlbaum Associates, 2012).

CHAPTER THREE

~

Conceptualising Why
Education Matters

In the English language, the term 'education' can be used to cover a range of practices, from the more elementary forms of instruction to the relatively complex, socio-cultural practices involved in attaining a professional identity. The most inclusive conceptions are not so useful for my purposes; we need, for example, to distinguish education 'proper' from the broader processes of socialisation. For although socialisation is clearly an important dimension of education, it lacks the element of intention that characterises educational institutions and relationships. That is why we can talk of educators, but not socialisers – the 'active agent' in socialisation being the anonymous collective whose processes are mostly non-conscious and mimetic – and why we can use the term 'educational' to hint at something more than socialisation.

This is not to say that education is always formalised in school-like settings consisting of teachers and students. As mentioned in the introduction, I find value in certain conceptual distinctions that are lacking in the English language but available in the vocabulary of the Nordic and German *pädagogik* tradition. For example, the formal education taking place in schools and universities would be called *Ausbildung* in the German language, but I would also like to elucidate another meaning of the word education which in German is called *Bildung*. *Bildung*[1] refers to the cultural formation and self-formation of personhood or subjectivity.[2] The word education also covers what in German is called *Erziehung* (bringing up a child). Importantly, in all these cases there is a specifically educational *relationship* at work, where someone has a conscious *intention* to educate someone else. This relationship is asymmetrical, especially when children are concerned, where one party (the teacher or parent) is more powerful, knowledgeable and hence more responsible than the other. The notion of an educational intention immediately brings up ethical questions such as who has the legitimate authority for being (called) an educator and on what basis, with what kind of means, we can justify interfering with another person in a formative way. Questions like these are rarely, if ever, raised in processes of socialisation.

Another term that is closely related, but not synonymous to education, is 'learning.' Education without learning is hard to imagine, and would certainly be rather useless, which is probably why policymakers see no problem in reducing 'education' to the more measurable term 'learning.' Learning, however, does not depend on an educational context but can and does take place in situations where any agent – such as an organism – interacts with its environment. In contrast to education, then, learning can be done without intention and by oneself. The concept of learning is used in animal psychology, in biology (bacteria can learn) and in computer science as machine learning. 'Education' clearly refers to something *more* than learning since it is possible to state that artificial neural networks can learn, but not that they are educated. In other words, when education is reduced to learning, something seems to be missing. This 'something more' is exactly what many theorists are trying to put words to as the most valuable (and elusive) aspect of education – and for some, bildung is that thing.

When asked, educators often state that their task is to bring forth *subjectivity* in others, such as the capacity to set aims for themselves, to adhere to reasons and develop interests of their own. Recalling the discussion about education being one of the 'impossible professions' in the previous chapter, it is not possible to simply plan, implement and *produce* subjectivity in others. For the subject or educated person is nothing like a result of input factors: as a minimum, for education to take place, the person in question must wish or at least agree to be educated by somebody else. And here is where the paradox of education connects explicitly to the notion of authority, first formulated by Kant.[3] The 'paradox' is that in order to develop the kind of freedom that we call autonomy (the ability to adhere to self-imposed laws or principles), a person must temporarily be under the authority of somebody else, the educator, and allow themself to be educated, to change and be changed.

In education, as Castoriadis observes in interview, we are "interacting directly with another individual's mind."[4] But "[t]here is no pedagogy," he continues, "if the pupil does not have any investment, in the strongest sense of the term, both in what she learns and in the learning process." In practice, this investment can only be made via a "concrete person, through a Platonic

Eros," as Castoriadis puts it.[5] Inside the relation of pedagogical authority, this concrete person/teacher acts as an object of projection and a proxy subjectivity for the student. Indeed, a teacher who is not capable of "inspiring love in children, love both for what they are learning and for the very fact of learning" is not really a teacher, for Castoriadis.[6] This love of knowledge and desire to learn outlives the relationship between student and teacher and becomes an ego structure of *autonomous* subjectivity or self-authority.

Genuinely educational relationships involve risk and trust, psychological investment and openness to the unknown. Importantly, though, education is more than a relationship. The Germanic tradition offers a model to illustrate this called the 'didactic triangle,' consisting of a *triad* between the teacher, the student and the knowledge or subject matter in which the teacher and student are both engaged. Inside this triad, the teacher-authority serves to direct attention and psychological investment for the young learner, while authority is gradually transferred from teacher to student as the capacity to gain knowledge and understanding. For example, as a university lecturer I might wish for my students to experience and appreciate the beauty of a theory or the importance of a philosophical question. They, on their part, might want to know the best and most efficient way to get a passing grade. In this situation, my job would be to make the theory and question *matter*, and hope that at least some of the students will find that it does, *to them*. From there on, I become more of a fellow traveller than a guide, all depending on the students' further engagement. For the teacher's authority – guidance and discipline – loses its function when the desire for knowledge is internalised as self-cultivation (or self-bildung). Without such investment, Castoriadis comments in the interview, schools may produce "whizzes at passing examinations" but fail to nurture "receptive individuals, open to the world, and passionately interested in knowledge, that huge dimension of human existence."[7]

This complicated notion of authority is characteristic for the impossible professions. The way autonomy is established 'paradoxically' through transference, calling forth a subjectivity that cannot be planned for, only hoped for, is easily overlooked when policymakers describe educational processes in simple terms such as 'knowledge,' 'skills' and 'learning outcomes.' Likewise, the way Castoriadis describes knowledge as "that huge dimension of human learning" echoes of something deeply meaningful for human existence, and not primarily something useful.

A somewhat different, but related description is offered by British philosopher of education Richard Pring, who, with reference to Michael Oakeshott, describes education as a "conversation between generations" that is mediated by "the voice of poetry, the voice of science and the voice of history."[8]

Leaving aside for now the problematic reference to voice in the singular, the quote elucidates how education may also refer to the awareness of a common world of significations, traditions and practices.

As I have already pointed out, my concern with education is not related to teaching and learning as such, but rather to the field of reflexive cultural and political praxis circumscribed by the term *pädagogik* and the philosophy of education. From this perspective, education is one of the fundamental institutions of modern societies that mirrors the concerns, norms and ideals of a given society, and also a locus or screen from which this society can reflect upon itself, its values, social hierarchies and direction. This *dual function of social self-representation and self-reflection* alludes to the sociological and political significance(s) of education, engaging with broader meanings than are found in common speech.

The term 'bildung' is often used (also in English) to designate this meaning of education.[9] As already signalled, I would like to apply the understanding that bildung offers, but since I prefer to use English vocabulary, I will now argue that a good basis for this understanding can be found in the concept of education itself, with reference to some important distinctions made by the pioneer of British analytic philosophy of education, Richard Stanley Peters (1919–2011).

Travelling with a Different View: Education as Bildung

In 1965, R. S. Peters set out to define and delimit the concept of education in ways that bring him quite close to the (Northern European) notion of bildung. Among Peters's interlocutors or opponents were those who treated education as a social or economic good to be invested in and/or distributed among those who did not possess it – without defining *what it was* that should be distributed. According to Peters:

> Perhaps one of the reasons why these economic and sociological descriptions of education can be misleading, if taken out of context, is that they are made from the point of view of a spectator pointing to the 'function' or effects of education in a social or economic system. They are not descriptions of it from the point of view of someone engaged in the enterprise.[10]

To Peters, sociological or economic conceptions of education are not descriptions of what educators do *qua* educators. Should educators take over these descriptions from other disciplines – sociology, economics or psychology – it could endanger their self-understanding and their practice as educators, he argues. But "[e]verything is what it is and not some other thing," Peters firmly establishes.[11]

To further circle in the concept's essence, Peters draws up some distinctions and criteria that I believe are still relevant. One distinction is that education cannot be reduced to training or instruction, even though these activities will normally be *elements* in a person's education. But as Peters points out, it is possible to be trained or instructed in almost anything – a point which he, as a good analytical philosopher, illustrates with an extreme example: "For both training and instruction might be in futile things such as opium-taking." Failing to see this distinction would violate what Peters sees as a central criterion for education proper, namely, "of being worth-while."[12] In the same way as it would be self-contradictory to claim that a person has been educated "and yet the change was in no way desirable,"[13] he argues that the term 'education' should only be used to designate something that is considered desirable and worthwhile. To illustrate his point, Peters quotes Alfred North Whitehead, saying that: "'There is a quality in life which lies always beyond the mere fact of life.' The great teacher is he," Peter declares, "who can convey this sense of quality to another, so that it haunts his every endeavour and makes him sweat and yearn to fix what he thinks and feels in a fitting form." Education provides "that touch of eternity under the aspect of which endurance can pass into dignified, wry acceptance, and animal enjoyment into a quality of living."[14] Clearly, education for Peters – as for Castoriadis – is a human enterprise associated with higher forms of living, or better and more precisely: with living *well.*

Education can thus be further distinguished from learning and socialisation by the normative connotations it carries. Again, as the full quote of R. S. Peters reads: "'Education' relates to some sort of processes in which a desirable state of mind develops. It would be as much of a logical contradiction to say that a person has been educated and yet the change was in no way desirable as it would be to say that he has been reformed and yet had made no change for the better."[15] His younger colleague Richard Pring refers to this idea as the "evaluative dimension" of education, which for Pring connects to education's central aim, namely, "to help people become more fully persons – to develop those distinctively human qualities and capacities that constitute 'being a person.'"[16] "What is distinctive about education," according to Pring, "are the connections it makes between the cultural inheritance, on the one hand, and the minds of the learners and the different ways in which they understand and appreciate, on the other." Accordingly, the aim of education is to "develop understanding of the world one inhabits, to act intelligently and humanely within it, and to contribute positively to the wider community one is part of."[17]

Still another criterion for Peters is that an educated person should be able to put what they learn into a larger perspective. This implies that education "should not be confined to specialist training," but rather the individual "should be trained in more than one form of knowledge."[18] Together with the former criteria, I find Peters's concept of education to be quite close to the concept of bildung, echoing as it were the words of Humboldt quoted in the previous chapter, namely that:

> It is the ultimate task of our existence to achieve as much substance as possible for the concept of humanity in our person [. . .] through the traces we leave by means of our vital activity. This can be fulfilled only by the linking of the self to the world to achieve the most general, most animated, and most unrestrained interplay.[19]

Overall, Peters's emphatic notion of education is not narrow and specific, nor is it all inclusive. His 'education proper' is not directed toward an extrinsic purpose of utility but is seen as valuable in itself, with its own internal standards and aims such as humanity or being a person. As Rebekka Horlacher writes about bildung: "It represents an unquantifiable excess value that ought to be administered in schools or at universities."[20] Similarly, for Peters, "'education' involves essentially processes which intentionally transmit what is valuable in an intelligible and voluntary manner and which create in the learner a desire to achieve it."[21] This means that education, for Peters, "can have no ends beyond itself. Its value derives from principles and standards implicit in it. To be educated is not to have arrived at a destination; it is to travel with a different view."[22]

Peters's essay is titled "Education as Initiation." With their classical and slightly elitist ring, his views have taken a beating over the years. What his analysis *does* achieve, nonetheless, is to defy instrumentalism on the one hand, and reductionism on the other, for example the tendencies to reduce education to its elements or processes, such as instruction or training, or more recently, to learning. He also demonstrates that education is a social practice, which Peters develops under the label of initiation into a culture with certain standards for thinking and for critique. Finally, his conception of education points toward a social-historical dimension: for what counts as valuable imaginaries at any given time is subject to historical change, and thus also to political considerations and valuations.

The drift toward economic terminology in educational policy has not diminished since Peters's time, on the contrary. For example, Jan Masschelein and Simon Maartens have vividly described how the notion of an "entrepreneurial self" has taken over in policy documents.[23] Similarly, Gert Biesta has identified what he calls a 'new language of learning' based on the logic of transactions, where learning is something that can be offered in a market and bought by 'learners' in the form of 'learning outcomes.'[24] This drift from education to learning has the effect of blurring distinctions and tends to relativise (and ignore) questions of contents and educational meaning.[25]

Irrespective of how convincing or dated we find Peters's views, I believe his analysis can help us see that the concept of education is richer, and more in line with bildung and *pädagogik* than what one might think when reading documents from the UN and the OECD. At any rate, it should now be relatively clear that the elements, contents and purposes of education are not uncontroversial conceptions that can be outlined once and for all. For example, what it means to be a 'person' at any given time and place is a question of historical and socio-cultural meaning and valuations. And likewise, what 'the voice' of poetry, science and history 'speaks' (Oakeshott) is not the same for all, but is quite different depending on our position in the social fabric. For where some hear wonderful tales of heritage and a glorious past, others hear superiority and dominion. In the normative sense alluded to by Pring, then, what counts as the "distinctively human qualities and capacities of a person" is certainly saturated with socially and politically contestable meaning. In other words, to be counted as 'educated' always means to be seen as a worthy member of a specific community and a social form in a given time and place on earth. Once again, we see that being educated is a question of the *social imaginary significations* (Castoriadis) which a society chooses to institute for itself as its world.

Education and the Power Apparatus

The previous section has highlighted an overwhelmingly positive conception of what education can mean in a person's life but also hinted at aspects of social hierarchy and control. This doubleness – the double significations of education and its dark underside, schooling – is well illustrated by a quote from Raymond Williams:

> The process of education; the processes of a much wider social training within institutions like the family; the practical definitions and organization of work; the selective tradition at an intellectual and theoretical level: all these forces are involved in a continual making and remaking of an effective dominant culture, and on them, as experienced, as built into our living, reality depends.[26]

Understanding the role of formal and informal education in the power apparatus is central for getting a grasp on how a society establishes and changes
itself. In democracies and dictatorships alike, institutions for qualification
and socialisation are needed – whether their aim is to foster autonomous,
self-reflexive citizens or flexible workers who ask as few questions as possible. Castoriadis refers to this dimension of the social as society's "ground
power" or "infra-power" through which a society exists and upholds itself
on a very basic level.[27] Schooling is certainly a most important part of this
ground power of society: through schooling and (largely) informal education,
individuals become 'selective embodiments' or 'walking fragments' of society,
carriers and often defenders of its central values, significations, norms and
social roles.

Schooling can further be seen as a distinctly modern phenomenon, whose
modes of organisation are rigged to produce power in the form of regulated
patterns – for example, when children are trained to wait for their turn, adhere
to commands and reproduce information as knowledge.[28] In contrast to clan
structures or feudalism where power is demonstrated explicitly and often violently, the instruments of state power in modern societies are less explicit than,
and operate in invisible ways, often internalised as modes of self-regulation.
However, with neoliberal reforms, Tomasz Szkudlarek observes, the power
element of schooling has actually returned to the public arena. Contemporary school systems, he notes, are organised around testing qualifications,
achievement and accountability – including sanctions for those teachers
and school administrators that fail to improve results. Education is therefore
one of the few places in modern societies where power is made visible. In
Szkudlarek's terms, children in modern societies are the "screens onto which
political subjection is projected."[29]

A significant distance can be observed between Szkudlarek's notion of
schooling as political subjection and R. S. Peters's notion of education as travelling with a different view. This tension, or conceptual doubleness, is a more
or less direct representation of society's instituting capacities making clear that
education is not neutral, but part of the power apparatus and at the same time
a possibility to reflect upon it.

From Means–Ends to Reflexivity

Sometimes one might think that a good political theory would become
perfect if accompanied by an educational agenda. Thoughtful policy makers would set the goals and professional educators could find the best means
to implement them. But, as a reading through the history of philosophy of

education will show, this instrumentalist vision – making 'education' the means for something else – is probably what is *most* resisted by philosophers of education. We saw it in Daniel Tröhler's notion of "educationalisation", in R. S. Peters, who refused to accept that education should be subsumed to some other domain such as economics or social science, and will see it again below when Gert Biesta's work is discussed.

The threats of instrumentalism are diverse, and the term can also be used in various ways – here, I will focus on how educational matters are reduced to a question of means and ends, where education becomes pure means.[30] The means-end-logic is often close at hand since the most common justification for education and schooling is that children need to learn certain things, develop skills, knowledge, habits, and so on, in preparation for adulthood and to participate fully in society. However, this truism immediately raises the question of what kinds of knowledge, skills and values are legitimate and necessary to learn in schools, and who should decide in these matters, on which grounds.[31] The central question here is whether these questions belong to the educational domain or to some other profession.

Philosophers of education since antiquity have pointed out that instrumentalism in education reduces a field of *praxis* to a set of techniques crafted to achieve purposes or aims that are given in advance, from educations' outside. This approach goes against what many educators identify with as being educators: it violates their professional ethos and the reasons why they have chosen their profession. Being an educator is not the same as fulfilling the plans of the OECD or the ambitions of national authorities. This is not to say that educators want to be the sole experts or decision-makers when it comes to the purposes, aims or contents of education: rather, it means that the very separation of 'ends' and 'means' leads to a poor understanding of both these concepts. But when education is seen as techniques or means to an end, educators are turned into functionaries or technicians whose only decisions are how to find the most efficient means, without formal opportunities to reflect upon education's purpose, justifications or deeper kinds of questions that are arguably inherent to the praxis of education. This kind of teacher could, as history shows, be a dangerous person.

One of the most unwavering critics of instrumentalism in contemporary education is Gert Biesta. Like Amy Gutmann (whose theory will be discussed in chapter 4), he is concerned with "who should be allowed to participate in decisions about what is educationally desirable" and argues that these questions should be directed to society as a whole, and not, as is increasingly the case, experts in evidence-based education.[32] A narrow focus on techniques and efficiency, Biesta argues, risks leaving out the more important questions of which "ends and means" are seen as *educationally* desirable. One of his fears is that educationists (educational theorists), through policy processes, are being made into "handmaidens" for political philosophy. Another concern is that educators are expected to simply execute evidence-based policies of "what works." Importantly, for Biesta, educators (practitioners and theorists) should be allowed to address technical questions about education "in close connection with normative, educational, and political questions about what is educationally desirable." Indeed, the extent to which a government not only allows, but "actively supports and encourages researchers to go beyond simplistic questions about 'what works,'" he argues, "may well be an indication of the degree to which a society can be called democratic."[33]

Biesta's call to broaden the debate about what education is and what it should be for means to politicise it. Like Peters before him, he speaks for *educational* reflections rather than extrinsic (instrumental) standards. However, Biesta also takes into account the power dimension of schooling that was left out by Peters (cf. the previous section). For this and other reasons, a closer look at Biesta's theory is interesting for our discussion.

Subjectification as a Political Dimension of Education: Gert Biesta

Over the last two decades, Gert J. J. Biesta has been probably the most important European educational theorists in terms of his originality and influence. A highly productive scholar, his work has been especially significant to the Western and Northern parts of Europe where his ideas and conceptual apparatus have been taken up by educational scholars and practitioners alike.[34] As a sign of his theoretical ambition, Biesta penned "A Manifesto for Education" in 2011 together with the Swedish educationist Carl-Anders Säfström.[35] This manifesto, which has been followed up in later works, is a good place to start to explore his thoughts about how politics and education are connected.

The central concern of the manifesto is the notion of education: what it means and what it ought to mean. The authors start out by noting that there are "a number of ways of speaking and doing and thinking about education [circulating] in society at large and in the field of educational research [that] run the risk of keeping out or eradicating the very thing that might matter educationally."[36] In other words, the authors see a need to distinguish and speak up for an education proper:

> This manifesto is an attempt to articulate what it might mean to speak for education in a way that recognises what it is that makes education special, unique and proper. In this regard the manifesto aims to identify the challenges

that need to be met if one wishes to stand up for education – which means to stand up for the possibility of freedom.[37]

By associating education with the possibility of freedom, then, Biesta and Säfström's manifesto presents itself as an emancipatory project. Their plea for education as a project with its own aims and internal standards follows in the footsteps of R. S. Peters, for, as noted by philosopher of education Robin Barrow, "it was Peters who most obviously made and acted upon the point that if education is the name of our game, then it is on the idea of education itself that we ought to focus."[38]

The ambition shared by Peters, Biesta and Säfström is to defend education proper from being colonised, occulted, or exploited by other kinds of logic, especially instrumentalism and economic policies. But where Peters used formal concept analysis to decide on the central or constitutive characteristics of the concept of education vis-à-vis contingent, peripheral, or irrelevant notions, Biesta (and Säfström) is not interested in conceptual clarification as such.[39] In order to identify the aspects of education that are under threat, Biesta instead employs a genealogical approach that is *not* directed toward education as such, but toward notions of teaching and learning. His approach is eclectic and decidedly postmodern, drawing elements from sources as different as John Dewey, Michel Foucault, Jacques Rancière and Hannah Arendt. Much of Biesta's work also carries rather strong existentialist undertones from Emmanuel Lévinas and Jacques Derrida that come to expression especially when he formulates his own alternatives.[40]

An example from the manifesto concerns the contrast the authors draw between education seen as an activity "directed at the future" and a "pedagogy for the here and now." The authors note that education, since the Enlightenment, has been conceived as "a process aimed at the realisation of freedom," and that such freedom is often "projected into the future" – either through a psychological focus on development from child to adulthood or through a sociological focus on "social change, liberation from oppression and the overcoming of inequality." "In this way," they remark, "education has not only become tied up with progress but has actually become synonymous with it." However, the authors contend,

> by conceiving education in terms of what is not yet – that is, by conceiving education as a process that will deliver its promises at some point in the future – the question of freedom disappears from the here and now and runs the risk of being forever deferred. This locates the educational in a place beyond reach.[41]

But *the educational*, they argue, is found in the tension between "what is" and "what is not," which is "the place where subjectivity comes into the world." This "place" is later developed into the notion that Biesta calls *subjectification*, which comprises a central "domain of educational purpose," as well as a political dimension in Biesta's theory of democracy. Biesta's effort to bring 'the political' explicitly into educational theory, along with the emancipatory orientation, is my main reason for giving his ideas considerable space – despite a number of inconsistencies, as we shall see. But I will start with one of his most important and influential achievements: the critique of learnification.

The Regime of Learnification

Gert Biesta first became an educational hotshot when he picked up, and named, a new trend in educational policy at the beginning of this century. Then, Biesta acutely perceived the concrete ways in which education was transformed from a public good into a commodity, which meant that education was being pushed into "a logic of production, that is, of predictable connections between 'inputs and outputs.'"[42] Starting toward the end of the previous century, universities in the Anglophone world, South-East Asia and elsewhere started to compete intensely for students in a higher educational market. In Europe, major initiatives for lifelong learning like the Bologna process and the Lisbon Strategy caught Biesta's attention with their declarations that learning was now something that was necessary for all, and that Europe would become a leading region in the promotion of lifelong learning. With his novel, and critical, terminology and phrases such as "the learner identity" and "the new language of learning," Biesta rung the bell for educators who felt that their motives and reasons for being educators had here been given a voice. In later works, these analyses have coalesced into the social diagnosis of *learnification* with a genealogy that effectively pinned down some of the far-reaching effects of neoliberal transformations in the educational sector, including the meaning and significance of learning, teaching and of education itself.

The "learnification" of educational discourse and practice represents, for Biesta, a tendency to talk about education exclusively using what he calls a "language of learning."[43] In nation after nation, the new language of learning replaces all other, for Biesta, more *educational* concepts, for example when children, pupils, students and adults are retitled as 'learners,' or when schools, libraries, universities, etc., are turned into 'learning environments' and 'places for learning.' The main problem with learnification, according to Biesta, is its inherent instrumentalism where education becomes 'pure means': "The problem with the language of learning is that [it] refers to processes that are 'empty' with regard to content and purpose. So just to say that children should learn or that teachers should facilitate learning, or that we all should be lifelong learners, actually says very little—if it says anything at all."[44] What is missing, according to Biesta, is attention to "questions of content, purpose and relationships." But when learnification replaces education proper, such questions are occluded, and we are left with the assumption that "the only relevant content is academic content, that the only relevant purpose is academic achievement, and the only relevant relationship is for teachers to train students so that they generate the highest possible test scores, for themselves, their school, and their country."[45] Not surprisingly, the language of learning fits hand in glove with systems for control by measurement, accountability and competition.

Biesta is not alone on making this diagnosis. In a similar but more Foucauldian critique, Maarten Simons and Jan Masschelein depict how learning is increasingly seen as a form of capital for which the learner is made personally responsible.[46] The social type of today is, they argue, is an "entrepreneurian self" who manages themself as an investment. In the "learning society," *learning to learn* represents a new form of hyper-flexibility where content in effect becomes irrelevant. Consequently, the learning individual, the *learner*, can never be certain whether they have reached their learning goals – for the goals always change, or move further ahead, so that learning – and the accompanying self-monitoring and insecurity, the need to perform without knowing exactly how – is indeed lifelong. In the neoliberal regime of learnification, flexibility is like an obligation where individuals, deprived of job security and predictability, are under the duty to learn, a duty clad in the terminology of freedom, flexibility and self-realisation.

The empty goals of neoliberal education have little in common with classical liberal education, according to French sociologist Christian Laval. Where classical humanism or liberal education had goals such as the formation of an autonomous personality, capable of reasoning and dignity, neoliberal education (or rather, schooling) resembles the training of a sportsman, or the "hyperconnected stock speculator" who keep their eyes glued to performance tables "where their physical or financial investments are displayed."[47] The introduction of economic language, metrics, systems for documenting and controlling just about everything is clearly alienating for teachers who see their professional autonomy and judgement ignored and rendered irrelevant. In this respect, learnification is part of a much larger trend of neoliberal governance, including benchmarking, responsibilisation of individuals and best practices – a neoliberal regime which, according to Wendy Brown, serves to occlude collectives and transform individual subjects into replaceable elements.[48]

Interestingly, Biesta observes that learnification is a process of depolitici-sation whereby "political problems, such as questions about the economy and about social cohesion, are turned into learning problems, and . . . individu-als are subsequently tasked to contribute to the solution of these problems through their learning."[49] To resist this tendency, he argues, individuals must resist and denounce the learner identity itself. He then draws the somewhat surprising conclusion that learning *as such* is the problem, making the case for a kind of teaching disconnected from learning which he calls a "pedagogy of the event," orientated toward "the weakness of education."[50] The purpose of this pedagogy is to "open up other existential possibilities for our students, other ways for our students to be in and with the world – particularly ways that allow for the world to encounter us and address us, so that it can appear in its own right rather that only as an object of our comprehension."[51] The model teacher for Biesta's "weak education" is "the ignorant schoolmaster" (from Jacques Rancière) – a 'teacher' without knowledge, authority or tradi-tion; and he advocates 'education' as the ability to be touched by teaching. I will not follow this line of reasoning, which offers little in terms of political understanding, but instead focus on Biesta's own political alternative, which he calls "subjectification." But first, I will briefly consider a few problems with his approach to learnification.

Biesta's Aporias

I share many of Biesta's educational beliefs and concerns, notably his care for subjectivity formation (or what he calls "subject-ness"), his interest in the significance and meaning(s) of education, and more specifically the way he treats education as essentially oriented toward democracy, politics and the world. That said, I can only follow him part of the way. So far, Biesta's work has received little philosophical critique, but two of his prominent critics are Marianna Papastephanou and Thomas Aastrup Rømer, whose analyses of Biesta will be referred to in the following.

The first problem, addressed by Papastephanou, is how he totalises and overstretches the learnification diagnosis. In order to "interrupt the politics of learning," Biesta emphasises the need to reject learnification and 'the learner identity.' He also advocates a pedagogy of "obstinacy" and resistance, as illustrated by titles like "Against Learning" (2004/2005), *Beyond Learning* (2006) and *Obstinate Education* (2019). However, when his 'resistance' turns against learning as such, Biesta runs into aporias. Rather than singling out a specific form or learning under neoliberal governance, for example, with terms like "what passes as learning in our time,"[52] Marianna Papastephanou comments, "Biesta wants to free teaching from learning but he does not want (or does not consider it possible) to free learning from learnification."[53] Likewise, instead of differentiating between different kinds of learner identities, Biesta maintains the "One learner identity" – "as if the learner identity should be incriminated for the content that it takes in western vocabularies."[54] But by reducing the issue to "an either/or (either we decide not to learn or we 'succumb to the duty to learn')," Biesta becomes "trapped in the drastic choice that this dilemma imposes," as Papastephanou duly notes.[55]

Biesta's refusal or failure to differentiate between learning as an essentially *neutral* process – as shown by Peters, almost anything can be 'learned' – and the *neoliberal deployment* of the term where subjects are shaped according to, and internalise the logic of, numbers and quantification,[56] has further led him to reject some of the more political or politicising perspectives on education that have emerged over the past decades: theories that might have served as alternatives to individualistic, cognitivist and biologist learning theories.[57] However, by rejecting learning (and, oddly enough, also bildung),[58] Biesta distances himself from more collective conceptualisations of what it means to learn. As we shall see next, his theory is firmly placed inside an ontological individualism.

"Only Individuals Can Learn"

When educational thinkers in the 'sociocultural tradition' from around the 1980s, inspired especially by Lev Vygotsky, turned their attention toward the 'learning environment' – a concept firmly rejected by Biesta – it served several critical purposes.[59] By putting the learning subject at the centre of education, instead of the teacher, teaching methods or the curriculum, the sociocultural perspective on learning presented itself as a more egalitarian, student-centred approach. Part of the rationale behind this shift of perspective was that educational processes without 'learning outcomes' for the student could not rightly be called 'education.' But more importantly for our discussion, and for thinkers in the sociocultural tradition, was the philosophical reorientation of education itself, from the individual's interior – the brain's cognitive structures – to cultural practices.[60] In short, the sociocultural perspective on learning was an epistemological and ontological turn toward socially instituted meaning.

However, one of Biesta's reasons for turning 'against learning' is that learning, as he sees it, is a concept that refers to individuals, which for him means that by using the term 'learning' we turn people into individual learners. For Biesta, learning does not – cannot – refer to the collective level because, as he states in several places, "after all, it is impossible to learn for somebody else."[61] This seems to be a very curious basis for classifying learning as individualistic: for in making this statement, he has already made individuals the unit of analysis in an atomistic, un-relational way ("learning for somebody else"), and in extension, since it would also be impossible to be educated for somebody else – and the same can be said of most human activities – an individualist ontology setting individuals as the primary unit from which everything else stems seems unavoidable. I find this critique both untenable and strange. Strange, because the relevant question is not whether it is possible for one individual to learn *for* somebody else, but whether collectives can know and learn something *as collectives*. In saying that learning only refers to individuals learning *for themselves*, Biesta ignores the possibility of any broader notions of learning and knowing, including organisational learning, distributed cognition, social imaginaries, collective representations and a range of other kinds of knowledge-meaning that exist as embodied by collectives, groups, organisations and societies. In other words, through this much-repeated statement in Biesta's oeuvre, he firmly subscribes to an ontological individualism where knowledge is something that exists in somebody's head performed for oneself.

Another notion that is lost by Biesta, then, is social meaning and social imaginary significations. This blindness is intensified by his conceptualisation of the social, which for Biesta exists exclusively as structures, rigidity, order.[62] Inside his poststructuralist framework – which in this respect is curiously close to political liberalism – all notions with positive value (freedom, change, emancipation) are located at the level of the individual.

Having rejected learning as the most central notion in education, one might have expected that Biesta would turn toward the other educational core concept in European educational thought, namely *bildung*. In the Scandinavian context, for example, learning and bildung have historically been the two pillars of higher education, and up until World War II bildung was the only really important aim in Nordic teacher education.[63] A self-reflexive notion of bildung might have taken care of many of the problems identified by Biesta, and helped to shed light on how the discourse of learnification has drained education of its raison d'être: the formation of subjectivity. But Biesta chooses to set himself aside from bildung, which he considers to be too associated with modernist ideals such as rational autonomy based on "a general or universal perspective" that he thinks has become problematic in the "postmodern world."[64] In so doing, he has actually become the foremost critic of *both* bildung and learning. Thomas Aastrup Rømer questions why Biesta has abandoned the bildung tradition that would seem to rhyme so well with central parts of his thought, finding that Biesta here misses an opportunity to engage with "a fruitful educational paradox" and runs into aporias again.[65] However, there is a reason why Biesta does not turn to bildung, since he has his own alternative to the learner identity, namely, his concept called 'subjectification,' to which we now turn.

Citizenship: Social or Political

Democratic citizenship education is the main orientation of Biesta's more political thought, developed especially in *Good Education in an Age of Measurement* from 2009/2010[66] and *The Beautiful Risk of Education* from 2014. In the latter, Biesta sets out to distinguish between what he sees as two different concepts of citizenship: a "social identity" and a "political" conceptualisation. His starting point is a scheme that has been used and reused many times since 2009, outlined as three "domains of educational purpose." These domains, which apply to formal (institutionalised) education, are called *qualification*, *socialisation* and *subjectification*.

The domain of qualification, in one of its typical renderings, concerns "the ways in which, through education, individuals become qualified to do certain things." Qualification is often formulated as "the acquisition of knowledge, skills, values and dispositions." The next domain of purpose, socialisation, refers to "the ways in which, through education, individuals become part of existing social, political, professional, and other 'orders.'" Third, he outlines the domain of subjectification, "which, in opposition to socialisation, is not about how individuals become part of existing orders, but how they can be independent – or, as some would say, autonomous – subjects of action and responsibility."[67] I will return to these definitions in more detail below.

The distinctions between the three domains is a political matter for Biesta, as shown in the way he orients his definitions around the term *order* from Jacques Rancière in the following. Biesta explains:

> While qualification and socialisation can contribute to the empowerment of individuals in that they give them the power to operate within existing socio-political configurations and settings, subjectification has an orientation towards emancipation – that is, towards ways of doing and being that do not

simply accept the given order, but have an orientation towards the change of the existing order so that different ways of doing and being become possible.[68]

On various occasions, Biesta defines subjectification negatively in contrast to socialisation. While socialisation concerns the process of becoming "part of existing traditions and ways of doing and being – an identity determined by the social – subjectification is a process whereby students can be(come) subjects in their own right and not just remain objects of the desires and directions of others."[69]

Subjectification is by far the most interesting domain for Biesta. In *The Beautiful Risk of Education*, he refers to "the interest of education in the subjectivity or 'subject-ness' of those we educate" in terms of "emancipation and freedom" and "the responsibility that comes with such freedom."[70] Although he points out that there is no inherent hierarchy between the three domains of educational purpose, he also underlines that without an interest in subjectification, education runs the risk of becoming "just another instrument of social reproduction."[71] In other words, subjectification contains a political quality that the others are lacking, which connects education to the instituting, socio-creative dimensions of politics.[72]

Even though all domains are said to be important, Biesta argues that there are inherent problems in how education is often reduced to the dimensions of qualification and socialisation. Importantly, for him, education as socialisation does not provide a proper connection between private and public concerns, nor does it challenge the existing socio-political order. In its place, Biesta wants to promote an understanding of citizenship that is:

> more political than social, more concerned about collective than individual learning, [an understanding] that acknowledges the role of conflict and contestation, and that is less aimed at integration and reproduction of the existing order but also allows for forms of agency that question the particular construction of the political order.[73]

This reorientation is underscored by the need to acknowledge "that the social and the political understanding of citizenship are not the same" and should not be conflated.[74] Stressing the need to "acknowledge the political 'foundation' of democratic politics," Biesta here makes a case for conceptualising politics, in a strong and explicit sense, in educational thought. His theory of citizenship, *subjectification*, will be discussed in detail further below. First, let us see what Biesta has to say about the political dimension of democracy. The logical place to look would be his definition of democracy, which in its "shortest formula," for Biesta, "is about learning from difference and learning to live with others who are not like us. For this very reason democracy can only be learned *from* life," he contends.[75]

It is of course remarkable that the most prominent critic of the ubiquity of *learning*, Biesta, defines democracy primarily in terms of learning (three times in two short sentences), and not, for example, in terms of self-governance or self-institution (Castoriadis), decision-making and deliberation (Jürgen Habermas, John Rawls) or legitimate struggles over power (Chantal Mouffe). Part of the explanation is probably that Biesta wants to coin an *educational* notion of democracy (I will have more to say about this below). But a more immanent problem is that Biesta's conception of democracy as "learning to live with others who are not like us" is still, despite his declared intentions to the opposite, a *social* conception of democracy. I find nothing of a political nature in the definition, such as political causes (the 'what' of politics) or the notion of questioning or challenging existing powers. In fact, living together with our differences is something that can be done in a society where politics has *not* been instituted, such as a digital environment governed, in all political respects, by corporate logic, like a Brave New World. Biesta's definition is suited for life in the classroom, but in my opinion it fails to capture the *political* aspects of democracy. In this respect, Biesta comes close to Dewey's pre-political conception of democracy as "primarily a mode of associated living, of conjoint associated experience" (a discussion of Dewey will follow in the next chapter). And indeed, in another work from 2006/2007, Biesta himself endorses a social conception of democracy over a more political one, for the following reasons:

> A *social* conception of democracy acknowledges that democracy is not exclusively about collective decision making in the political domain, but [. . .] has to do with participation in the 'construction, maintenance and transformation' of social and political life more generally [. . .]. A social conception of democracy expresses, in other words, that democracy is about inclusive ways of social and political action.[76]

By emphasising a "social" conception of democracy, Biesta claims to have captured a "democratic intention," thus widening what he sees as a narrow conception of democracy (i.e., democracy as a form of government and collective decision-making), with explicit reference to Dewey. He thereby succeeds in criticising instrumentalism in educational policy, but only at the cost of sacrificing democracy as a political form of rule, that is, self-government.

In another context, Biesta turns to Chantal Mouffe and Jacques Rancière, noting that political activity is first and foremost about the constitution of a political order, but that this kind of order never can be permanently established in a democracy. 'Democracy' is therefore something that per definition escapes every attempt to determine its (particular or universal) form. The establishment of a political order is for Biesta essentially a question about who – what kind of whos – constitutes this order. With reference to Rancière's notion of order, Biesta then sets forth his notion of "subjectification," as the "coming into presence" of "a way of being that had no place in the existing order of things. Subjectification is therefore a supplement to the existing order because it adds something to this order, and precisely for this reason the supplement also divides the existing order."[77] The idea is that when somebody makes themself present, counted among those who count, the (democratic) order is renewed and altered every time. This analysis thus offers two alternative identities for citizens: either as individuals socialised into the existing social order or as subjectivities who make themselves existent as political events.

Increasingly, in later works, Biesta's main concern is democratic subjectivity or "subjectification," a notion he constructs from rather different sources. Starting in an article from 2003, he criticises the idea that the task of educational theorists would be to work out programmes for educating citizens in accordance with the needs of political theorists, something which would have turned educationists into "handmaidens" for political philosophy. Instead, he proposes to view democracy as an educational problem in its own right, where the main purpose for democratic education would be to support, or call forth, subjectivity.[78] Against this background, he proposes the following "educational definition" of democracy: "Democracy is the situation in which all human beings can become subjects," which means "to create a situation where all have the same right to participate, and are equally entitled to be heard in questions of common interest."[79] Having established that Biesta endorses (ambiguously) a social conception of democracy focusing on inclusion and the question of who should be heard, we will now take a closer look at notion of subjectification.

Subjectification and Socialisation: A False Opposition

In "Interrupting the Politics of Learning," Gert Biesta defines "the domain of subjectification, which, in opposition to socialisation, is not about how individuals become part of existing orders, but how they can be independent – or, as some would say, autonomous – subjects of action and responsibility."[80] And he continues:

While qualification and socialisation can contribute to the empowerment of individuals in that they give them the power to operate within existing socio-political configurations and settings, subjectification has an orientation towards emancipation – that is, towards ways of doing and being that do not simply accept the given order, but have an orientation towards the change of the existing order so that different ways of doing and being become possible.[81]

Subjectification for Biesta includes a rejection of the learner identity and becomes a position *beyond* learning. Somewhat reluctantly, he alludes to autonomy, not in the sense of collective and individual self-governance but, rather, in the liberal meaning of independence from social structures: "how they can be independent – or, as some would say, autonomous – subjects of action and responsibility." Echoing, as it were, the atomised and free-floating neoliberal subject, Biesta's subjects have no provisions for their subjectivity in the social, and no social resources exist except as negation, because for Biesta, traditions, institutions and society can only be seen as rigid structures. In his analysis there are only individuals (and their relations) on the one side and structures on the other, with little or no room for theorising institutions or the collective imaginaries they embody. Through this abstraction, Biesta ends up, according to Rømer, on a path "leading into identity-politics."[82]

An alternative and more consistent view on the relationship between socialisation and subjectification would be that subjectification is made possible through a *certain* kind of socialisation, namely the kind that aims at emancipation, or with Castoriadis: individual and collective autonomy. For as I have already elaborated in detail, socialisation can be of different kinds, depending on the type of society and how it has instituted itself. What Biesta seems to overlook, then, is that socialisation *can* also be of the kind that promotes or enables subjectification. I find Castoriadis convincing when he states that "[i]ndividuals become what they are by absorbing and internalizing institutions," and that this internalisation "is anything but superficial: modes of thought and of action, norms and values, and, ultimately, the very identity of the individual as a social being all depend upon it."[83]

If this idea is plausible, and if subjectification is to be a possibility, then the resources for subjectification are either obtained from a transcendental source or somehow drawn from the instituted society where subjectification is instituted as a possibility (such as a social imaginary signification). This is perhaps the most important point where Biesta's perspective becomes insufficient, politically speaking. For in order to think politically (Gauchet) we need to look at how different societies have instituted themselves *differently* from each other. This insight is also crucial for theorists of education in a democracy, where the differences between autonomous and heteronomous forms of self-institution are far from trivial.

To sum up: Biesta, as we have seen, has set forth important questions and a powerful critique of learning society/learnification. His political programme is to conceptualise and promote an education that makes questioning of the social institution possible. Regarding his socio-political ontology – his resources for theorising politics and the political – it consists of two poles: one is the pole of individual identities or subject positions, and the other consists of structures in the most rigid, inflexible sense of the term. His political aim is to educate subjects who are capable of challenging the social order; however, he does not acknowledge that the resources for their subjectivity are in and of the social, but instead locates them somewhere "beyond" the instituted society, in the "here and now" or the "unexpected." At this point, Biesta's theory leaves the worldly life of politics and education behind.[84]

Freedom, described as independence from structures and from socialisation is the core value in Biesta's and Säfström's educational manifesto; while subjectification, the situation where everyone can become subjects (without learning), is described as an existentialist leap. However, without a concept of institutions, the subjects' freedom remains abstract. A more productive and practical approach would be to consider how institutions can be questioned and recreated through activities involving experiences with action and power that allow for subjectification.

The way Biesta reserves learning (and education) for the individual further leads him to ignore collective learning processes that are characteristic (political) theories of social learning, such as eco-literacy, critical eco-pedagogy and so forth. By restricting his optics to individuals versus structures, he further ignores the social movements that are central in radical politics and critical pedagogy. His examples are usually taken from the classroom and the teacher-student relationship in the singular. Most crucially, what he fails to see is that different institutions offer and open up for *different forms of socialisation* and hence for subjectivity. Since Biesta's political analysis lacks attention to the different ways a society can institute itself – for example, as different kinds social meaning – and for all the other listed reasons, his most political thought turns out to be remarkably apolitical in the end.

Why Autonomy Is an Individual and Collective Project

As the discussion of Biesta has shown, a socio-political ontology consisting only of individuals and structures is very problematic from a politico-democratic viewpoint. Natalie Doyle provides a relevant context to this problem in her description of two lines of post-Marxism in French political philosophy: one represented by Michel Foucault, Jean-François Lyotard, Jacques Derrida and others, and the other by Cornelius Castoriadis, Claude Lefort and Marcel Gauchet. For the latter group, she notes that the "essentially political nature of human societies" originates in imaginary and symbolic processes "which produce specific visions of the world and, with these visions, specific configurations of social organisation and political power."[85] Neoliberal societies can serve as examples, with their specific subject positions (the entrepreneur), their logic, language and ordering of the social. The opposite view, that societies are nothing but the sum of individuals and their intersubjective relationships, choices and sentiments, constitutes "the essence of neoliberal economism" according to Gauchet.[86]

However, the admittedly more influential line of post-Marxism, loosely called post-structuralism, postmodernism and/or identity politics – seeing only power in structures and unable to grasp the productive, collective power of the social-historical imaginary – fails to engage with this symbolic, imaginary dimension that is first and foremost made explicit in institutions.[87] Instead, Doyle comments, "the idea that the existence of a symbolic order underpinning social life negates or fundamentally constrains human freedom" has come to characterise the Nitzschean post-structuralism or "radical form of scepticism" represented, especially, by Foucault. Gert Biesta's educational theory is a clear example of this post-Nietzschean – limited and limiting – perspective that has become enormously influential in Northern Europe and elsewhere over the past decades.[88]

I believe we are now ready to understand why autonomy, following Castoriadis, *must* be seen as a phenomenon that is collective and individual at the same time. The simple point here is that autonomy for individuals – or its possibility as reflexive subjectivity and political citizenship – is instituted in the social in the form of a political democracy. Autonomy is above all a political notion of freedom that is (or is not) instituted as meaningful for the members of a society. It is *not* a question of gaining independence from structures (a notion that is almost meaningless for Castoriadis) but an acknowledgement that we need to build structures that can foster freedom for its members *as far as possible*. Castoriadis's theory further underlines how the freedom of one person depends on freedom of others, and that society's institutions, including socialisation (society's infra-power), are prerequisites for the effective realisation of freedom. Most importantly, I want to emphasise the need to see freedom as a 'real' signification and not some kind of lack, or mysterious leap.

But even though freedom is something that is (or is not) instituted as meaningful, it is essential to note that autonomy for Castoriadis cannot be instituted once and for all. Individual and collective autonomy is a historical project and a continuous struggle for a flexible and conscious relationship between the instituting and the instituted society. Since 'instituting society' refers to "the social imaginary in the radical sense," it is never completely captured or fixed in the instituted society.

Castoriadis uses the term 'heteronomy' to designate a society that has closed itself off against its own instituting processes. Heteronomy and closure is for him the most common state toward which every society tends to drift. In a society that has instituted itself reflexively – I avoid the term 'autonomous society,' which suggests a state to be attained permanently rather than an enduring project – this drift toward heteronomy is openly recognised and challenged. If the "project of an autonomous society [is] to succeed," Castoriadis writes in an article from 1997, it "has to establish a democratic society."[89] The aim, however, is not to fulfil a certain ideal – autonomy as a philosophical standard – but much more important, for Castoriadis, an ability to act. For "[a]utonomy is not just an end in itself: we want autonomy for its own sake, but also in order to be able and free to do things."[90]

The cycle of questioning and self-institution is perpetual: its goal is not a perfect society, but one that is as free and as just as possible. The "struggle for autonomy," then, is a historical project, "the emancipatory project to which both democracy and philosophy belong."[91] Contemporary efforts to create chaos in the political domain can be seen as direct attacks against this sort of explicit self-institution, where misrecognition and distrust based on disinformation make political democracy difficult. As Noam Chomsky observes in one of his many video talks, there is an on-going "epistemicide" that aims at making our societies ungovernable by attacking our ability to form collective convictions. To be sure, for the sake of autonomy and freedom, we need to be able to conceptualise collective forms of meaning and action as something more than "order" and "structures."

Notes

1. Most of the time, I have spelled 'bildung' with lower-case 'b,' but here I refer to the German language explicitly, where nouns are capitalised.

2. Bildung is sometimes contrasted to *Ausbildung*, and in the Scandinavian languages: dannelse to *ut*dannelse, bildning to *ut*bildning, etc. The prefixes Aus-, ud- and ut- all mean the same thing, namely 'out,' alluding to the notion of education bringing somebody out of a state, as in the Latin concept of *educare*.

3. See Alexander Von Oettingen, *Det Pædagogiske Paradoks*.

4. Castoriadis, "Psyche and Education."

5. Castoriadis, "Psyche and Education," 178.

6. Castoriadis, "Psyche and Education," 179.

7. Castoriadis, "Psyche and Education," 179.

8. Richard Pring, "Philosophical Issues in Educational Research: An Overview," in *Encyclopedia of Educational Theory and Philosophy, vol. 2*, ed. D. C. Phillips (London/Thousand Oaks: SAGE, 2014), 619.

9. See, e.g., Lars Løvlie and Paul Standish, "Introduction: Bildung and the Idea of a Liberal Education," *Journal of Philosophy of Education* 36, no. 3 (2002).

10. R. S. Peters, "Education as Initiation," in *Philosophy of Education: An Anthology*, ed. Randall Curren (Oxford: Blackwell, 2007), 56.

11. Peters, "Education as Initiation," 56.

12. Peters, "Education as Initiation," 62.

13. Peters, "Education as Initiation," 57.

14. Peters, "Education as Initiation," 67.

15. Peters, "Education as Initiation," 57.

16. Pring, "Philosophical Issues," 619.

17. Pring, "Philosophical Issues," 619.

18. Peters, "Education as Initiation," 62.

19. Wilhelm von Humboldt, "The Theory of Bildung."

20. Rebekka Horlacher, *The Educated Subject and the German Concept of Bildung* (London: Routledge, 2016), 3.

21. Peters, "Education as Initiation," 63.

22. Peters, "Education as Initiation," 67.

23. Maarten Simons and Jan Masschelein, "The Governmentalization of Learning and the Assemblage of a Learning Apparatus," *Educational Theory* 58, no. 4 (2008).

24. Gert J. J. Biesta, "Against Learning: Reclaiming a Language for Education in an Age of Learning," *Nordic Studies in Education* 24, no. 1 (2004).

25. Ingerid S. Straume, "'Learning' and Signification in Neoliberal Governance," in *Depoliticization: The Political Imaginary of Global Capitalism*, ed. Ingerid S. Straume and John F. Humphrey (Aarhus: NSU Press, 2011).

26. Raymond Williams, quoted in Michael Apple, *Ideology and Curriculum*, 3rd ed. (New York: RoutledgeFalmer, 2004), 5.

27. Castoriadis, "Power, Politics, Autonomy."

28. Tomasz Szkudlarek, *On the Politics of Educational Theory: Rhetoric, Theoretical Ambiguity, and the Construction of Society* (London: Routledge, 2016).

29. Szkudlarek, *On the Politics of Educational Theory*, 58.

30. This is *not* the kind of instrumentalism endorsed by John Dewey. Instrumentalism as the term is used here is a problem for educators, but also a problem for political thought. As Hannah Arendt argues in *The Human Condition* and *On Revolution*, instrumentalism as means-end-logic in the political sphere is destructive of politics itself.

31. See, e.g., Amy Gutmann, *Democratic Education: With a New Preface and Epilogue.* (Princeton, NJ: Princeton University Press, 1999).

32. Gert J. J. Biesta, "Why 'What Works' Won't Work: Evidence-Based Practice and the Democratic Deficit in Educational Research," *Educational Theory* 57, no. 1 (2007): 6.

33. Biesta, "Why 'What Works' Won't Work," 22.

34. As of 2022, his work has been translated into 20 languages.

35. Both are central at the Centre for Public Education and Pedagogy, https://www.maynoothuniversity.ie/centre-public-education-and-pedagogy

36. Gert Biesta and Carl Anders Säfström, "A Manifesto for Education," *Policy Futures in Education* 9 no. 5 (2011): 543.

37. Biesta and Säfström "A Manifesto for Education," 542, §7.

38. Robin Barrow, "Schools of Thought in Philosophy of Education," in *The SAGE Handbook of Philosophy of Education* (London: SAGE, 2010), 16.

39. I shall focus mostly on Biesta, as Säfström develops his thinking mainly with reference to the former. For example, in Säfström's book *A Pedagogy of Equality in a Time of Unrest: Strategies for an Ambiguous Future*, in all his closer readings of Rancière – the central theorist for Säfström – Biesta is the main source. For this and other reasons, Biesta stands out as the leading thinker in the group connected to the Centre.

40. See Biesta's intellectual autobiography in *Obstinate Education*, appendix: "From Experimentalism to Existentialism," 145–61.

41. Biesta and Säfström, "A Manifesto for Education," 541.

42. Biesta, *Obstinate Education*, 157.

43. Gert J. J. Biesta, "Freeing Teaching from Learning: Opening Up Existential Possibilities in Educational Relationships," *Studies in Philosophy and Education* 34, no. 3 (2014): 234.

44. Biesta, "Freeing Teaching from Learning," 234.

45. Biesta, "Freeing Teaching from Learning," 234.

46. Simons and Masschelein, "The Governmentalization of Learning."

47. Christian Laval, in interview, http://seer.upf.br/index.php/rep/article/view/12804; https://doi.org/10.5335/rep.v28i1.12804

48. Brown, *Undoing the Demos*, 129, 138, see also 175ff.

49. Biesta, "Freeing Teaching from Learning," 236.

50. Biesta, *The Beautiful Risk*.

51. Biesta, "Freeing Teaching from Learning," 242.

52. Marianna Papastephanou, "What Lies within Gert Biesta's Going beyond Learning?" *Ethics and Education* 15 no. 3 (2020).

53. Papastephanou, "What Lies within Gert Biesta," 282.

54. Papastephanou, "What Lies within Gert Biesta," 289.

55. Papastephanou, "What Lies within Gert Biesta," 293.

56. Christian Laval and Francis Vergne, *Éducation Démocratique: La Révolution Scolaire À Venir* (Paris: La Découverte, 2021).

57. Sociocultural learning theories have emphasised the activity of collectives, distributed cognition and organisational learning. I would include theories of eco-literacy and radical eco-criticism under the same heading.

58. G. J. J. Biesta, "How General Can Bildung Be? Reflections on the Future of a Modern Educational Ideal," in *Educating Humanity: Bildung in Postmodernity*, ed. Lars Lövlie et al. (Oxford: Blackwell, 2003). For a good discussion about Biesta's relation to bildung, see Thomas Aastrup Rømer, "Gert Biesta – Education between Bildung and Post-structuralism." *Educational Philosophy and Theory* 53, no. 1 (2021).

59. Examples from this tradition are Roger Säljö's sociocultural learning theory, Lave and Wenger's situated learning, Engeström's and Wertch's activity theory and Barbara Rogoff's cultural pedagogy.

60. Vygotsky is called a 'cultural-historical psychologist.'

61. Here is one example: "The fact that 'learning' is an individualistic and individualising term – learning is, after all, something one can only do for oneself; it is not possible to learn for somebody else – has also shifted attention away from the importance of relationships in educational processes and practices, and has thus made it far more difficult to explore what the particular responsibilities and tasks of educational professionals, such as teachers and adult educators, actually are." Biesta, "Interrupting the Politics of Learning," 6.

62. This stark dichotomy is constant with Biesta, according to Rømer, "Gert Biesta – Education between Bildung and Post-structuralism."

63. Tove Aarsnes Baune, *'Den Skal Tidlig Krøkes': Skolen i Historisk Perspektiv*, rev. ed. (Oslo: Cappelen Akademisk forlag, 2007); Ingerid S. Straume, "'Learning' and Signification in Neoliberal Governance.

64. Biesta, "How General Can Bildung Be?," 390.

65. Rømer, "Gert Biesta – Education between Bildung and Post-structuralism."

66. Gert J. J. Biesta, *Good Education in an Age of Measurement: Ethics, Politics, Democracy* (Boulder, CO: Paradigm, 2010). There is a journal article from 2009 with the same title as this book.

67. Biesta, *Good Education in an Age of Measurement*, 19f.

68. Gert J. J. Biesta, "Interrupting the Politics of Learning," *Power and Education* 5 no. 1 (2013): 6.

69. Biesta, "Freeing Teaching from Learning," 235.

70. Biesta, *The Beautiful Risk of Education*, 4.

71. Biesta, *The Beautiful Risk of Education*, x.

72. In "Freeing Teaching from Learning," on the other hand, Biesta states that there should be a balance between the domains of purpose, and that they may limit or disturb each other (235). Indeed, as Thomas Aastrup Rømer points out, Biesta constantly vacillates in these matters.

73. Biesta, *Learning Democracy*, 44. In this passage, Biesta endorses collective learning. As far as I know, this endorsement has not been followed up in other writings (although Biesta is so productive, with numerous overlapping publications,

that I have not studied them all), but instead, he defines learning as something that individuals do for themselves, as I discuss further below.

74. Biesta, *The Beautiful Risk of Education*, 2.

75. Biesta, *Learning Democracy*, 70. Biesta rarely uses definitions, but prefers to comment on what practices like democracy, socialisation, qualification and subjectification "are about."

76. Biesta, "Why 'What Works' Won't Work," 4.

77. Biesta, *Learning Democracy*, 95.

78. Biesta, "How General Can Bildung Be?," 64.

79. Biesta, "How General Can Bildung Be?," 65.

80. Biesta, "Interrupting the Politics of Learning," 6.

81. Biesta, "Interrupting the Politics of Learning," 6.

82. Rømer, "Gert Biesta – Education between Bildung and Post-structuralism," 42.

83. Castoriadis, "Psychoanalysis and Politics," 133.

84. See also Elodie Guillemin, "An Investigation of Education as Subjectification: Biesta's Use of Example" (MA thesis, Faculty of Education, University of Oslo, 2022).

85. Natalie Doyle, *Marcel Gauchet and the Loss of Common Purpose: Imaginary Islam and the Crisis of European Democracy* (Lanham, MD: Lexington Books, 2018), xxi.

86. Doyle, *Marcel Gauchet and the Loss of Common Purpose*, xxi.

87. Doyle, *Marcel Gauchet and the Loss of Common Purpose*, 1.

88. Rømer, "Gert Biesta – Education between Bildung and Post-structuralism."

89. Castoriadis, "Democracy as Procedure," 5.

90. Castoriadis, "Psychoanalysis and Politics," 134.

91. Castoriadis, "Psychoanalysis and Politics," 131.

CHAPTER FOUR

~

Political Imaginaries of Democracy and Citizenship

As we saw in the previous chapter, education and schooling can be seen as the 'ground power' of a society that forms its members while upholding itself as a meaningful form. Depending on the sort of regime, the educational system can both be the mirror where a society can reflect upon itself and the screen upon which its power structures are projected (Szkudlarek). I have also suggested that in a democracy, this ground power needs to be legitimate, and its schooling system as reflexive as possible. But what does this mean in more specific terms? It is time to take a closer look at how democratic imaginaries relate to specific educational conceptions such as citizenship and to visit some of the different approaches to education in a democracy.

Once more I would like start from Aristotle's observation that the education of the young is the prime task for a government (the lawgiver), and that "[i]n states where this is not done, the quality of the constitution suffers." There are, as Aristotle points out, inherent connections between the character of a people and the kind of regime they inhabit, which means that different types of regimes (πολιτείας) require different types of education producing, as it were, different social types who in turn represent the regime they inhabit.[1] In Aristotle's terms, "the democratic character preserves a democracy, an oligarchic an oligarchy" and so forth.[2] The relationship between (a certain type of) mind and (a certain type of) society goes two ways for Aristotle. The first refers to the socialisation process whereby a specific form of government fosters a corresponding character, and the second to the way individuals reproduce the social institution. However, according to

Castoriadis, "it would be erroneous to say, as some do, that society produces individuals, which in turn produce society." Rather, for Castoriadis, "society is the product of the *instituting* imaginary. The individuals are made by the *instituted* society, at the same time as they make and remake it."[3] This nuance makes it possible to see that society is also created, not by individuals as such but by the social creative capacity that he calls the "instituting imaginary." Accordingly, for Castoriadis, "the two mutually irreducible poles" are not the individual and the society, but

> the radical instituting imaginary – the field of social-historical creation – on the one hand, [and] the singular psyche, on the other. Starting with the psyche, using it, as it were, as a material, the instituted society each time makes the individuals – which, as such, can henceforth only make the society which has made them.[4]

Here we find the main logic behind why only reflexive institutions can foster reflexive subjects. The point may seem trivial and hardly worth labouring – but the truth is that this insight is exactly what neoliberal rationality aims to conceal. According to the neoliberal credo, and in much of contemporary philosophy, individual subjects are referred to as something more or less *independent* of society's structures, and the opportunities for individual freedom are effectively posited as society's *opposite*, as we saw in the previous chapter with Gert Biesta's domains of qualification, socialisation and subjectification. In other words, many contemporary theorists fail to acknowledge the fact that the resources for individual freedom – and the lack of it – are social. But as Aristotle and Castoriadis point out, all states, even neoliberal ones, are inhabited by subjects that correspond to the specific collective imaginaries of those societies. There is no escape from the fact that citizens of the Western world *are neoliberal subjects*, whether we like it or not. One of the begging questions, then, is whether there are sufficient (social imaginary) resources for producing democratic subjectivity under neoliberal conditions, or in other words, whether the ground power of contemporary democracies supports social reflexivity.

More than most other regimes, democracy depends on the members' will to endorse and practice its central values and imaginaries. Since the instituted, explicit power in a democracy needs to be legitimate, democracy requires the kind of socialisation whereby the instituted imaginary significations of democracy are *experienced* as one's own, infused with a (strong) sense of personal and collective meaning. For democracies can only exist as long as their members value and defend democracy's specific imaginaries, such as political freedom, equality and self-governance, but they are also *tragic* regimes in the sense that they can degenerate and even destroy themselves. As Castoriadis observes, even "a 'perfect' democracy," should such a thing exist, "will not be able to endure for more than a few years if it does not engender individuals that correspond to it, ones that, first and foremost, are capable of making it function and reproducing it." His conclusion is that "[t]here can be no democratic society without democratic *paideia*."[5]

What does this mean in practical terms? First of all, it means that society's members recognise themselves as *citizens* with a certain, public mind-set, and not only, for example, as consumers with private interests or persons with certain rights. In other words, a certain level of interest among the citizens for political questions and causes is needed for a democracy to function as a *political* regime. For as Wendy Brown, author of *Undoing the Demos*, notes, "[c]itizens cannot rule themselves, even if that means only thoughtfully choosing representatives of voting on referenda, let alone engaging in more direct practices of shared rule, without understanding the powers and problems they are engaging."[6]

Over the past two centuries, Brown asserts, public education in Western nations has been rigged to accommodate democratic self-rule; but this democratic purpose is now actively eroded by the way neoliberalism – defined as a governing rationality based on market values and metrics – reshapes our self-understanding. Under neoliberalism, the human subject is configured as "self-investing human capital," while education is directed at "human capital development" aimed to "maximise competitiveness." These priorities, Brown argues, run counter to democratic purposes and effectively serve to "undo the *demos*."[7]

But what does it mean when Brown says that citizens need a certain "understanding" in order to rule themselves? One interpretation could be that citizens cannot *justifiably* rule themselves – or rule *well* – without some political understanding, knowledge and engagement in political causes. This idea can also be found in Castoriadis's contention that "[m]ajority rule can be justified only if one grants equal value, in the domain of the contingent and the probable, to the *doxai* of free individuals," and that for this justification to take place, "the permanent labor of the institution of society must be to render individuals such that one might reasonably postulate that their opinions all have the same weight in the political domain."[8] What Castoriadis seems to imply here is that everyone's opinion is not equally valid *per se*, without some kind of qualification, but that a democracy needs (a certain level and kind of) public education in order to be politically legitimate. As

I will argue at the end of this chapter, the logic of right-wing populism does not acknowledge this principle.

An obvious element in an education for democratic citizenship worthy of the name is the ability to take a larger – public – perspective, for example through argumentation (giving reasons) and deliberation. Mechanisms that are rigged for deliberation, for example in groups or public fora where different interests and viewpoints meet, will serve to refine opinions and turn them into common concerns. Through processes of questioning, argumentation and exchange of viewpoints, partial or private interests can give way to public concerns that in turn can be formulated as propositions and, importantly, accepted as justified. Being able to say that "these are our laws" – and being willing to defend them as ours: the principle of self-binding – is perhaps the most important principle in a democracy. However, as Jürgen Habermas insists, for an agreement to be justified de facto, deliberation needs to be done in practice, not by proxy or in the form of declarations.[9] In other words, a truly political democracy needs to be experienced and enacted through real, active participation. Hence the importance of arenas for political exchange and interaction and procedures for collective self-binding.

Another aspect of Brown's assertion that citizens need to understand the problems and powers they are engaging is the idea that, without sufficient education, the electorate is vulnerable to political manipulation. As Brown comments:

> If democracy does not require absolute equality, but cannot survive its opposite, the same is true of an educated citizenry. Democracy may not demand universal political participation, but it cannot survive the people's wholesale ignorance of the forces shaping their lives and limiting their future.[10]

A rather disturbing onslaught in this respect took place when the US presidential election in 2016 was subjected to massive campaigns with false/misleading information from Putin's Russia. The so-called Kremlin papers revealed how American voters were manipulated via Facebook and other channels to have Donald Trump elected as the president of the United States.[11] Surely, when active steps are taken to confuse voters and promote political chaos, from a foreign state in this case, the demands on voters have drastically increased from the duty to stay informed to the much more difficult task of defying manipulation. For a democracy whose citizens are unable to, or worse, do not even care about distinguishing between truth and lies, will easily self-destroy.

Democracy and Its Tensions

I have now identified some rather general factors that seem important for democratic education: psychological investment in democracy's instituted meaning, legitimacy of arrangements such as the majority principle, mechanisms for public deliberation and self-binding and care for knowledge and truth. As I have shown in earlier chapters, similar imaginaries are also implicit in the notion of an education proper.

But what *is* a democracy? The term itself is full of tensions, which makes it difficult to outline its educational principles unequivocally, in detail. In the words of Pierre Rosanvallon:

> There is scarcely another word in political usage whose practical definition is more variable. Hence the recurrent tendency to prop it up with some adjective or other. Like an insipid dish that has taste only when spiced up, democracy has no real character except when it is specified that it is "liberal," "popular," "real," "radical," or "socialist."[12]

The internal tensions of the term, he argues, make it difficult to draw clear dividing lines between democracy and its pathologies "such as demagoguery or populism." But the problem runs deeper for Rosanvallon. The word 'democracy,' he says, "is at once a solution and a problem. In it coexist the good and the vague."[13] These conceptual difficulties are neither trivial nor solvable, according to Rosanvallon:

> This coexistence [of the good and the vague] does not principally stem from democracy's status as a distant and utopian ideal upon which everyone agrees, with disputes over its definition pertaining only to questions of the means for realizing it. Far from corresponding banally to a sort of methodological indeterminacy, the fluctuating meaning of democracy reflects its history and its essence, inextricably mixing the question of popular sovereignty with that of equality.[14]

There is an inescapable, central tension in modern conceptions of democracy, which for Rosanvallon sits between popular sovereignty and equality. In a similar way, Chantal Mouffe identifies the tension to be between popular sovereignty versus liberal rights. The tension(s) between popular sovereignty on the one hand and mechanisms to secure equality or rights on the other has developed over centuries of (mainly European) history: many of which saw no regime in existence that called itself 'democratic.'[15]

The common form of democracies in advanced capitalist societies are of a *liberal* and *representative type*, where the principle of popular sovereignty (self-governance) is mediated and indirect.[16] Their historical development involves historical struggles and compromises propped up by legal and political thought from the Roman republican tradition (which was not democratic). Importantly, the modern liberal state with its division of state powers, (more or less) market control and other 'checks and balances' has been rigged to protect democracy against being overthrown, for example, by an arbitrary majority. Among the more recent developments are various rights to protect and recognise minorities – which is also where we find many of the most heated political struggles of today.

It is also important to keep in mind that the development of modern forms of democracy went hand in hand with the development of capitalism, which has its own political dynamics, not least the accumulation of capital and oligarchic power in the form of dynasties and multinational corporations. An additional dilemma of modern democracies, then, concerns the tensions and contradictions between democracy and capitalism, as I discussed in chapter 1. One example is economic *inequality*, which makes capitalism thrive, at least up to a certain point, while posing a serious threat to democracies. This and other tensions represent a problem for democracy more than for capitalism, though, since the latter is quite capable of co-opting democratic imaginaries into its own logic without changing in any fundamental way.

Modern democracies, then, are subject to both 'constitutive' tensions between the different rationalities of the state, the economy and civil society and a more general erosion of political meaning. As already mentioned, since a democracy can only work as long as it is seen as legitimate – fair and just, with leaders that can be trusted – citizens must be engaged in *more* than elections: In the longer run, democracy must be *experienced* as the regime of explicit self-institution and freedom.

One of the initiatives to measure the state of contemporary democracies is the "Varieties of Democracy Research Project" (V-Dem), involving 50 social scientists and more than 3,500 country experts on six continents. V-Dem distinguishes between five "high-level principles" of democracy: *electoral, liberal, participatory, deliberative and egalitarian*.[17] These formal and non-formal factors are used as indicators of how nations are governed in practice. For example, nations classified as autocracies (states with elected, but authoritarian, leaders) may have an electoral system in place but nonetheless score poorly on people's self-rule. At the moment of writing, the number of democratic states scored by these parameters is at its lowest in 30 years, as a growing number of democratic nations today are becoming autocracies.[18] Indeed, it would seem that the short period where democracy was on the rise across the world, holding, as it were, a global promise, is over.

At least some of the problems experienced by contemporary democracies can be attributed to educational factors – for example, in cases where the value of knowing something about a political matter is seen as irrelevant for having an opinion about it (the lack of psychological investment in the distinction between qualified and non-qualified opinions), or when large portions of a population see themselves as not entitled to having – or voicing – a political opinion.[19] Another factor could be that educational systems are rigged increasingly as production systems valuing performativity, efficiency, entrepreneurship, and so forth, to the detriment of the question of education's purpose, such as democracy.[20] There are also tendencies to outright discredit the value of education and knowledge, notably in right-wing populist movements, which will be discussed further below.

For now, let me conclude that modern, liberal democracy is a regime riddled with tensions and that tensions can be difficult to handle in practice, but also – potentially – politically productive. When searching for what would be a worthwhile approach to democratic education in today's situation, I believe a visit to the first democracy could provide a fresh eye on what democracy might (also) mean in terms of citizenship.

The First Democracy: Rule by the People

The first known government that called itself a democracy was established in Athens, and is often dated to the reforms of Cleisthenes in 508–507 BCE. These reforms erected a rather intricate system for administering the affairs of the city.[21] Scholars of antiquity have argued that it was this administrative system – more than the people's assembly, which existed elsewhere and prior to the reforms – that made Athenian democracy so radical and efficient.[22] The reforms of Cleisthenes were explicitly set up to prevent aristocratic tribes from appropriating political power, first of all by reorganising the population of Attica into ten artificial tribes (the *fyle*) assembled by villages (*demes*) drawn from the whole region, thereby replacing the principle of heredity with politics. The new tribes were military units led by elected generals (*strategoi*) that significantly strengthened Athens as an expansive military power. The 139 Attican *demes* were legal, military and religious units of their own. They disposed a proportionate quota of councillors, which meant that even the remotest village took part in the affairs of the city.

Every year each of the ten *fyle* assigned 50 of its citizens to the important political-administrative function called the Council of 500 (the *boule*). Most

Athenian citizens from the age of thirty could expect to serve once during their lifetime. The most important task of the council was to draft the deliberations (*probouleumata*) for discussion and approval in the assembly (the *Ecclesia*). The council also directed finances and held important administrative and military functions. One of the important details was the so-called *prytany* system whereby each tribe presided over the council for a tenth of the year. Every proposition or case presented for the assembly was prepared by this group of 50 citizens, who served for 30 days and then never again.

The 'little man' also had his time: every day, all year round, a new person was selected by lot to hold the state seals and the keys to the treasuries and official archives and was, in effect, the city's chief executive officer. Since this position could only be occupied once, more than half of the Athenian citizens held this position during their lifetime. The *prytaneis* stayed in a special round house that was closely protected, since setting and preparing the agenda was considered a most important function of governing the city. To further prevent the concentration of power – oligarchy and tyranny – many important positions of public office were rotated among the citizens. All these intricate arrangements were designed to prevent corruption and also ensure that citizens were empowered to a degree that is hard to imagine for citizens of a modern democracy. Of course, it would not have been possible to be so involved in the running of the city without slaves and women to take care of day-to-day affairs such as production, housekeeping and various forms of labour.

The assembly consisted of all free citizens (males), and at Cleisthenes's time, the number of eligible male Athenians was set at 30,000.[23] Since all the political decisions and legislation were made by the assembly, the citizens were expected to stay informed. For this reason, the open public space (*agora*) where citizens could discuss political affairs *before* deliberations in the assembly was no less important to the *polis* than its formal organs. As Castoriadis underscores, the creation of a public space represented the creation of "free speech, free thinking, free examination and questioning without restraint."[24]

Supported by formal arrangements such as "*isegoria*, the right for all to speak their minds, and *parrhesia*, the commitment for all to really speak their minds concerning public affairs,"[25] the first democracy created the citizens, the *politis*. In contrast to some modern versions of democracy, *polis* and the *politis* were not seen to be in conflict, but as one and the same phenomenon, as also reflected by the fact that the ancient Greek word for 'Athens' and 'Athenian' was the same (*Athenai*). Indeed, Castoriadis emphasises that the substance of a democracy *is* the citizens: "Only the education (*paideia*) of the citizens as citizens can give valuable, substantive content to the 'public space.'" This *paideia* is an ethos, a shared responsibility: "First and foremost, it involves becoming conscious that the *polis* is also oneself and that its fate also depends on one's mind, behavior, and decisions; in other words, it is participation in political life."[26]

Meeting in the assembly, taking turns in administration and jury service were time-consuming activities that came on top of citizens' duty to fight in Athens's many wars at the time.[27] At all times, a large portion of the population was involved in public administration, the assembly, the Council of 500 and the juries,[28] and there were sanctions for those who did not take part in the running of the city, the so-called *apoleis*. Critics of modern versions of direct democracy often point out that since it is so time-consuming, it should be inefficient. But the fact is that the direct democracy of Athens was very efficient – Athens in the fifth and fourth century BCE was a very successful imperial power that won many wars.[29] In the end, though, Mogens Herman Hansen argues that the high degree of involvement and demands on the citizens made the first democracy kneel under its own weight.[30]

The First Citizen: Freedom through Self-binding

The first democracy had many arrangements to secure equality in participation – but not for everyone, since the freedom enjoyed by citizens depended heavily on slavery and the severe limitation of women.[31] Nonetheless, up until the collapse of ancient democracy in 322 BCE, the category of who could be counted as citizens was expanded several times. There is no continuous line from Greek to modern democracies, and the Greek citizen was definitely a very different social type than the modern voter. Still, I want to suggest that there are lessons to be learned from classical democracy, not least from how they treated educational and political questions. Indeed, it is possible to imagine that the Greeks of antiquity could have posed many questions to us that would make us more capable of self-government, less disengaged and perhaps also more optimistic about a common future.

A good place to start such an investigation is in Castoriadis's elucidation of classical (Athenian) democracy in texts like "The Greek *Polis* and the Creation of Democracy." Castoriadis sees the Greek democracy as an invention, or a creation, that is a "germ" of its modern forms. By this he means that even though the first democracy is not a model that modern democracies can emulate, there are certain imaginary significations and modes of understanding that are still active in how we evaluate democracies – and more generally, the project of autonomy – to this day. These imaginaries are also capable of functioning as a certain kind of standard that we may call, with a slightly adapted notion from Reinhart Koselleck, *self-stabilising concepts*.[32]

Self-stabilising concepts are normative or regulative concepts that endure over time by being questioned, renewed and reaffirmed in *new* forms. A most suitable example, also used by Koselleck, is bildung, or *paideia* in Greek antiquity. The German bildung tradition was established in the 18th century when the neo-humanists became fascinated by the way the Greeks valued and cared for their own education (*paideia*). Wilhelm von Humboldt, for example, saw in the Greeks an impulse – not to emulate Greek ideals, but instead to ask what the concept of *paideia*/bildung might mean for philosophers and educators in *his own* time. Seeing how the Greeks cared for and invested psychologically in self-education – through art, ritual and public arrangements – became an impulse for Humboldt to question what bildung means and what it ought to mean in a new, and different, time. The key idea here is that certain concepts serve as cultural norms by being reflexive, capable of being questioned, critiqued (can this really be called education?) and restabilised in forms that become new standards of judgement. Self-stabilising concepts, or reflexive imaginaries, are examples of how a culture (or a society) establishes its own standards through voluntary self-binding.[33]

In his study of Greek antiquity, Castoriadis goes a step further and argues that Western culture carries certain self-reflexive or critical traditions that were created with the Greek experience.[34] One of the central events in classical antiquity, an *invention* for Castoriadis, is the institution of politics. His basis for saying so is that even though all societies have a political dimension (French: *le politique*), not all societies have instituted politics (*la politique*).[35] The creation of a public sphere, which included the agora and the assembly, was crucial in this respect. The public sphere was clearly separated from the household (*oikos*), which was the domain of women and slaves.[36] The most distinctly public-political affairs were related to law-giving and decisions affecting the community/polis as a whole, such as whether or not to go to war – but in more general terms, Castoriadis defines politics as the *explicit activity of putting the established institution of society into question*, supported by arrangements for free speech (*isegoria* and *parrhesia*).[37]

Later forms of democratic polities have, to a greater or lesser degree, sought to embody the project of autonomy by instituting politics as the capacity of a society to question its own laws, norms and institutions, and especially its relations of power. It is exactly this instituted questioning or interrogation, for Castoriadis, that keeps a democracy alive and effective. In this sense, democracy is also a "self-stabilising concept": through processes of public scrutiny, listening, questioning, and deliberation, a political community may ask itself whether the thing that passes as a democracy is as democratic as to be worthy of its name – as indeed is being done in many contemporary publications, in books, online, in democratic experiments, social movements and so forth.

In contrast to modern forms of democracy, where education is formalised and often separated from other domains, education in the *polis* was inherent to the practice of self-rule, as Castoriadis observes:

> Rotation in office, sortition, decision-making after deliberation by the entire body politic, elections, and popular courts did not rest solely on a postulate that everyone has an equal capacity to assume public responsibilities: these procedures were themselves pieces of a political educational process, of an active *paideia*, which aimed at exercising – and, therefore, at developing in all – the corresponding abilities and, thereby, at rendering the postulate of political equality as close to the effective reality of that society as possible.[38]

The high degree of involvement in Athenian democracy ensured that the citizens were well informed and committed to the affairs of the city. In other words, every citizen's vote and opinion became *qualified through practice and experience*. Having experienced self-institution and self-government, the citizens knew that they, and their fellow citizens, were capable of ruling and being ruled. The public life of the polis was therefore an edifying project, captured by Plato's saying that the walls of the city are educators.

Citizen or Consumer?

The public/private distinction of classical times has been a challenge for modern theorists, where critics, especially feminists, have shown how it has been used to marginalise and exclude women's concerns and those of other underprivileged groups from the political agenda. Defining domestic violence as a family matter instead of a crime, for example, has been used to legitimise rape in marriage. But although the distinction can be drawn in problematic ways, there are good reasons of why it should not be abandoned. One of the ways the public/private distinction is politically relevant concerns the role of the citizen vis-à-vis the role of the consumer, where the two positions represent rather different domains of interest.

Philosopher Mark Sagoff has captured this difference very well when he admits that the political causes he supports seem to have little or no basis in his interests as a consumer because, he notes, "I take different points of view when I vote and when I shop."[39] His examples are as follows:

> I speed on the highway; yet I want the police to enforce laws against speeding. [. . .] I love my car; I hate the bus. Yet I vote for candidates who promise to tax gasoline to pay for public transportation. [. . .] I have an "Ecology Now" sticker on a car that drips oil everywhere it's parked.[40]

These different priorities are not a sign of inconsistency or weakness, Sagoff argues, but simply an expression of how the role of a citizen *transcends* the subject position of a consumer in assuming the position of a common 'we.' Considering the needs of a community, a society or the world as a whole leads us to taking very different perspectives than when we consider our own individual interests. In other words, people acting together in plurality – in the public sphere – have qualitatively different aims than private individuals. As consumers or private individuals, we have preferences, we desire, want or like certain things. This is what Charles Taylor calls *first order evaluations*.[41] But when we take the position as a citizen, we admit to second order evaluations, which implies second reflections: are these things that I want, also what I *ought* to want from a broader perspective?

Taylor's valuations of the second order is a type of questioning which, when transferred to the collective level, represents a mode of deliberation aimed at self-binding: where we adhere to regulations that we set to limit ourselves as a collective. Progressive taxes can serve as an example of a collective interest where a community may decide to limit economic inequality to prevent some being born into cycles of repeating poverty, for example by funding public education and healthcare through the use of progressive income taxes. However, the collective perspective, so central for upholding a political democracy, is difficult to maintain under neoliberalism, where increasing inequality is camouflaged as pseudo-meritocratic competition, and where citizens are increasingly called 'taxpayers' (by conservative parties especially). In contrast to the citizen, the taxpayer is a version of the consumer, this time the consumer who wants personal value for their tax money. Not much psychological insight is needed to understand why appeals to self-interest are more easily transmitted in the media than appeals to the self-binding citizen whose main interest is the good of the polis. In contrast to the first citizens – who were involved in public affairs whether they wanted to be or not – contemporary citizens may experience the need to *insist* on being addressed in that capacity.

Conceptions of Citizenship

I think it is correct to say that democracy theorists from antiquity to this day agree that democracy (in all its varieties) needs education. But what kind of education? Adhering to the chapter's starting point, Aristotle's thesis that the quality of a constitution depends on education (*paideia*), and given the long history of democracy theory, one would expect a great body of scholarly works on how educational theory relates to different conceptions of democracy and vice versa. And for some parts of the field this is true: when it comes to the theory of deliberative democracy and citizenship education, there is a considerable body of literature in circulation. This literature typically describes the various skills, knowledge, attitudes and competences that are seen as necessary for active citizenship, and how they can be developed and practiced in the classroom. Theories of deliberative citizenship, as the term is used here, typically draw ideas from John Dewey, Jürgen Habermas and John Rawls. Their underlying democratic ideal is liberal, deliberative and procedural, emphasising public will-formation, legitimacy, argumentation and critical reasoning skills.

Other smaller strands of citizenship literature include republican, cosmopolitan, critical and radical notions of citizenship, eco-citizenship and more. But the main contestant to deliberative citizenship theories today is probably *agonal citizenship* constructed around the political thought of Chantal Mouffe. One of the central ideas in agonal citizenship is that emotions, and conflict, are key ingredients in political engagement. In the choice between individual liberal rights and popular sovereignty, proponents of agonal citizenship always speak for the latter. An important aspect of their critique of liberal political theories of democracy and citizenship refers to the need to understand and engage young people in the political affairs of their time.

The next sections will outline, in a simplified way, what I believe to be the dominant theories of citizenship today and explore what they consider as politically relevant in education. All these theories arguably have some blind spots – but this is to be expected, given the ambiguities and tensions in the notion of modern democracy itself, as we have seen (Rosanvallon). We start out with the modern classic, John Dewey, who is still a central reference in the field.

John Dewey's Experimental Citizen

The first modern thinker who firmly re-wedded education to a political purpose was the great educational theorist, philosopher and psychologist John Dewey (1859–1952). Dewey was central in developing progressive, child-centred education and had a wide, international influence during his lifetime and up to this day, not least in the Nordic nations. He was an official educational adviser to Mexico and Turkey under Kemal Atatürk, and his ideas were taken up by Japan and China, where he spent two years.[42,43]

In *Democracy and Education*, from 1916, Dewey observes that a society that is interested in self-improvement takes a particular interest in the kind of education that aims to go beyond social reproduction and perpetuation of customs. Such a society will be oriented toward changing itself. Dewey, writing *Democracy and Education* during World War I, also saw it as important to avert socioeconomic hierarchies and class conflict since a society with too many 'sub-groups' is inherently unstable and unable to improve itself. His particular focus was on communication between different groups, arguing that groups who have restricted their communication with the outside are both "antisocial" and narrow-minded, because "isolation makes for rigidity and formal institutionalizing of life, for static and selfish ideals within the group."[44] A democratic society for Dewey, then, is one that is able to improve itself – but flexibility should not turn into instability. With this rationale, Dewey deduces two criteria[45] for how a society can handle rapid changes without being destabilised: 1) society needs to be open, and 2) it must have self-improvement as its ideal. Such a society fosters communication, internally and externally, through many points of contact and shared interests within and between different groups. These characteristics are also central for a democracy as he sees it:

> The two elements in our criterion both point to democracy. The first signifies not only more numerous and more varied points of shared common interest, but greater reliance upon the recognition of mutual interest as a factor in social control. The second means not only freer interaction between social groups [. . .] but change in social habit – its continuous readjustment through meeting the new situations produced by various intercourse. And these two traits are precisely what characterize the democratically constituted society.[46]

A large degree of openness and interaction will liberate people's potential to create and improve their conditions, including education. For a democratic community, having self-improvement as an ideal, will be more interested in "deliberate and systematic education" than other communities "have cause to be."[47] The close connection between education and democracy is "a familiar fact" for Dewey; however, the "normal" explanation for this connection, viz. that "a government resting on suffrage cannot be successful unless those who elect and who obey their governors are educated," is "superficial." This argument, he states, is based on the need to produce legitimacy: "Since a democratic repudiates the principle of external authority, it must find a substitute in voluntary disposition and interest; these can be created by education."[48] It was in order to step beyond this superficial argument for democratic education that Dewey made his memorable statement: "A democracy is more than a form of government; it is primarily a mode of associated living, of conjoint associated experience."[49]

Dewey's idea is that when a great number of individuals are engaged in various interests and activities that refer to each other, "so that each has to refer his own action to that of others, and to consider the action of others to give point and direction to his own," class barriers are broken down and society's democratic powers are liberated.

The "traditional" view on democracy, Dewey explained in a speech for his 80th birthday, "Creative Democracy – The Task Before Us" (1939), was "a kind of political mechanism that will work as long as citizens were reasonably faithful in performing political duties."[50] Politics itself was seen to take place somewhere else – at the state capital or in Washington – whereas for Dewey, real democracy relates to ordinary people's capacity for meaningful action, captured by the phrase "democracy is a way of life":[51]

> Democracy is a way of life controlled by a working faith in the possibilities of human nature. Belief in the Common Man is a familiar article in the democratic creed. That belief is without basis and significance save as it means faith in the potentialities of human nature as that nature is exhibited in every human being irrespective of race, color, sex, birth and family, of material or cultural wealth. This faith may be enacted in statutes, but it is only on paper unless it is put in force in the attitudes which human beings display to one another in all the incidents and relations of daily life.[52]

Typical democratic "attitudes," as he saw it, meant being inquisitive, explorative, creative and active – echoes of his philosophical position in pragmatist experimentalism. Dewey ended his speech by pointing to "the task of democracy" being "forever that of creation of a freer and more humane experience in which all share and to which all contribute."[53]

His strong emphasis on the democratic purpose of general/public education has made Dewey an enduring inspiration for educators across the world.[54] His concept of democracy as a *mode of living together* highlights how democracy's institutions cannot work according to their purpose without citizens who live and embody the imaginaries of democracy from early childhood. It is also a notion that can be translated to activities in the classroom with relative ease. Through his emphasis on the practical dimensions of what makes a democratic society work at its best, notably communication oriented toward solidarity, openness and tolerance, Dewey helped to bring democratic politics back, or down, to communities and different social groups. His more radical, political, and social motives related to class and race, however, have been toned down in the reception of his thought.[55] Accordingly, when Dewey's theory of democracy is limited entirely to "internal and external communication," "shared interests" and a "mode of associated living," as often happens in education, I find it to be unsatisfactory from a political perspective. What is lacking, in my view, is attention to political causes that may be divisive, and proper distinctions between the *social* and *political* aspects of democracy (we saw this problem with Gert Biesta in chapter 3 as well). Without such distinctions, Dewey's concept of democratic education becomes vulnerable to depoliticising trends and stands in danger of losing its capacity to foster political change. Nonetheless, Dewey has been an invaluable inspiration for everyone from social-democrats to post-structuralists and political liberals.

The Deliberative Citizen

We now turn to a set of theories that draw on John Dewey's ideas in addition to those of other theorists such as Jürgen Habermas and especially John Rawls.[56] The philosophical basis for theories of deliberative citizenship is in liberal political theory from the 20th century. When presenting this conception, we should consider the specific contexts where its central questions have developed, notably North America and the UK. As we shall see, some of the questions addressed by scholars like Amy Gutmann, Eamon Callan and Harry Brighouse are directed toward rather specific, political realities that may seem alien in other contexts. For example, from a Nordic, Scandinavian perspective where basic education is mainly public with a national curriculum, it is strange to read heated discussions about the degree to which parents or religious groups should be allowed to decide the school's curriculum or control the content of libraries (for us, not at all). However, some of the problems addressed by these theorists have become more acute over recent years, for example in current controversies over 'critical race theory' and representations of non-binary gender in (mainly Southern) parts of the United States with repercussions to other parts of the world.

In *Democratic Education*, Amy Gutmann posits what she sees as the "central question in the political theory of education," namely, "[h]ow should citizens be educated, and by whom?"[57] and similarly, "[w]ho should have the authority to shape the education of future citizens?"[58] In an argument that is analogous to John Rawls (in *Political Liberalism*) she explores what would be a *justified* approach to decide over the contents, aims and nature of education. Acknowledging that 'democracy' is a contested term, Gutmann goes for a minimal definition, where 'democratic' means to adhere to principles that are strictly public and therefore legitimate in the sense worked out by Rawls in the said work.[59] The political problem addressed by both stems from the notion that modern democracies consist of groups adhering to very different life-views who are competing for influence over society's institutions. Many of these life-views are incompatible, but nevertheless what Rawls calls 'reasonable,' and therefore their adherents claims to political influence are more or less equally legitimate. As he puts it:

> The political culture of a democratic society is always marked by a diversity of opposing and irreconcilable religious, philosophical, and moral doctrines. Some of these are perfectly reasonable, and this diversity among reasonable doctrines political liberalism sees as the inevitable long-run result of the powers of human reason at work within the background of enduring free institutions.[60]

This multiplicity of doctrines nevertheless represents a threat to society's integration. The task for a political theory, then, is to find out which basic institutions and principles can secure the existence of "a just and stable society of free and equal citizens, who remain profoundly divided by reasonable religious, philosophical, and moral doctrines."[61] More precisely, for Rawls, the aim of *politics* is to secure stability on the basis of principles and 'reasonable' conditions as worked out by *philosophy*. *Education*, in its turn, is charged with the need to foster citizens who do not challenge the democratic order but defend and maintain it.

There is in political liberalism an underlying fear that a random majority – a majority tyranny – should decide to dispose of democracy itself. Accordingly, many of its concepts stemming from the republican tradition – such as legal protection of minorities, mechanisms for equality in distribution of and access to resources, representation via political parties, and so forth – are emphasised to ensure that the people rule themselves *within reasonable limits*. Protecting the rights of minorities, for example, serves to limit majority decisions both in scope and contents. In other words, the arrangements of liberal democracy set limits to popular sovereignty and binds democracy in the liberal rule of law (German: *die Rechtsstat*). These mechanisms for self-binding should hinder a majority from abolishing democracy itself.[62]

One of the deeper questions, or tensions, in democracy theories is exactly how close the association should be between democracy and the liberal *Rechtsstat* should be. Chantal Mouffe and Jacques Rancière are two theorists who argue that democracy should have almost *unlimited* popular sovereignty, whereas liberal thinkers such as Rawls and Gutmann more or less identify democracy with the liberal rule of law and legal arrangements. Indeed, both the early and the late Rawls sought to restrict the unstable, unpredictable elements in democratic politics, as commented on here by Sheldon Wolin:

> Proceduralist politics, politics contained within and firmly constrained by agendas designed beforehand to assure what Rawls regarded as rational outcomes, emerges as the liberal alternative to the threat of destabilization implicitly attributed to participatory politics where structure and agenda are exposed to the vagaries of democratic decision-making.[63]

Amy Gutmann endorses Rawls's definition of what is at stake in a political democracy, namely integration of groups with differing and sometimes conflicting life-views. The notion of democracy in her *Democratic Education* is about procedures, balancing of rights, individuals versus society, differences in life-views and distribution between groups. She is also openly inspired by John Dewey.

For Gutmann, the central questions for a theory of democratic education include who controls the curriculum, whose values should be promoted, who ought to choose and, most importantly, on what basis these questions should be settled. Accordingly, the main objective of her theory is to develop institutional relations between different groups in society that are *just and legitimate*, which means to *exclude deeply political questions* such as what type of society is desirable (e.g., neoliberal capitalism, social democracy, socialism or something else). In fact, Gutmann warns us that the access to exert influence over education must be limited, in order that citizens do not destroy the foundations of liberal democracy itself:

> A democratic theory of education recognizes the importance of empowering citizens to make educational policy and also of constraining their choices among policies in accordance with those principles—of nonrepression and nondiscrimination—that preserve the intellectual and social foundations of democratic deliberations. A society that empowers citizens to make educational policy, moderated by these two principled constraints, realizes the democratic ideal of education.[64]

For our purposes, it is also interesting to see how Gutmann goes so far as to identify a society's degree of democracy with its concern for (public) education, which in turn means society's conscious reproduction: "A democratic theory of education," she says,

> focuses on what might be called 'conscious social reproduction'—the ways in which citizens are or should be empowered to influence the education that in

turn shapes the political values, attitudes, and modes of behaviour of future citizens.[65]

We see here an echo of Aristotle's idea about how citizens are both products and creators of a 'constitution.' The primary basis for conscious social reproduction, according to Gutmann, is the *citizens' capacity for deliberation*, which should be fostered through education.[66] Questioning is not ruled out, as critical and engaged citizens are seen as desirable; but the theory itself is geared toward stability and compromise.[67]

Notwithstanding how they sometimes present themselves, liberal-political principles are not without political presuppositions, but are based on specific conceptions about human nature and normative assumptions about the relationship between the individual, the society and the state. Its downside, which is noteworthy, is that deeper questions about, for example, what counts as legitimate grounds for decision-making are not up for dispute but are worked out philosophically, in advance. By blackboxing deeper questions, political thinkers such as Rawls and Gutmann are in effect placing limits on the space for questioning to predetermined 'fundamentals.' However, in all fairness, radical political change was never a stated aim in political liberalism. The guiding question in *Democratic Education* is who – or more precisely, whose interests – should be allowed to decide over the contents, aims and nature of education, and its objective is to develop just, institutional relations between different groups in society. Other, more difficult *political* questions, such as what type of society is desirable (e.g., neoliberal capitalism, socialism, ecological democracy or something else), are not part of the analysis.[68]

Liberalism and Curriculum Struggles

The perspectives of Gutmann and other liberal theorists have become very relevant in recent years, with an on-going political struggle over the curriculum in American public schools. In the US educational system – which is very different from Europe's – there are state boards of education, local school districts and individual schools that in various respects are involved in deciding about the curriculum. In many states, associations of parents and various (often religious) groups assert their rights to influence the contents of education and what counts as worthwhile knowledge. Two well-known examples from the 2000s are so-called intelligent design versus the theory evolution and whether students in school should be taught about anthropogenic climate change.[69] In the 2020s, another heated conflict emerged over the question of race and racism. Race conflicts, as George Packer convincingly argues,[70] have been underlying American politics for centuries, and are also inherent in the works of Dewey and Rawls. Currently, in the early 2020s, literature questioning racism – and equally heated, gender – is subjected to censorship in schools and their libraries. By July 2021 over 50 propositions had been discussed or proposed in 27 states to ban so-called critical race theory – originally an academic discipline from the 1960s. By February 2023, 18 states had imposed bans against teaching critical race theory, while another 44 had introduced bills to limit discussions about race and sexism in the classroom.[71] Some of society's deepest conflicts were thus placed at the level of schools, seriously challenging the public-private distinction that has been so central in a political democracy and at the same time illustrating the relevance of Gutmann's and Rawls's project.

Agonal Citizenship: The Citizen as Adversary

The deliberative approach to citizenship that has been dominant in educational departments for a long time resonates well with liberal theories of democracy, as we have seen. But a powerful critique has been building over the past decades based upon Chantal Mouffe's conception of the inherently antagonistic nature of politics. Mouffe is among the few political theorists who have coined an explicit notion of citizenship, developed in contrast to liberal and republican concepts. She first called her theory "radical democratic citizenship."[72] The more recent concept of 'agonal citizenship' takes most of its argumentation from her work from 2005, *On the Political*, where Mouffe develops her position with reference to Carl Schmitt's critique of liberalism in *The Concept of the Political*, from 1932. Mouffe, like Schmitt, upholds the idea that contestation, conflict and disagreement are constituents of the political field and as such should not be overcome or dissolved, but rather – and here she departs from Schmitt's authoritarian theory – channelled into democratic forms as "agonistic pluralism."[73] One of the political facts overlooked by liberals, Mouffe and her interpreters argue, is people's need to identify with groups or collectives, and by overlooking this need, they also ignore the role of emotions in politics.[74] Education for agonal citizenship is set forth to deal with *already existing diversity in democratic forms*, and therefore also to take problems like political disengagement seriously. For, as Mouffe and her followers see it, the mainstream, liberal approach to politics is disengaging and too far removed from the ways the political is lived and experienced.

Mouffe's approach is leftist and practical; but she does not suggest overthrowing the liberal democratic framework, which she finds flexible enough to be (re-)configured in a range of ways. In other words, she does not question the framework itself, only how it should be organised. For example, she endorses liberty and freedom for all and draws the limit for her agonistic pluralism at those who challenge the institutions constitutive of the democratic political association. Although the contents and shape of those institutions should be open for debate, Mouffe also believes that a "shared symbolic space" is necessary for legitimate, democratic confrontation. However, she contends:

> Instead of trying to design the institutions which, through supposedly "impartial" procedures, would reconcile all conflicting interests and values, the task for democratic theorists and politicians should be to envisage the creation of a vibrant "agonistic" public sphere of contestation where different hegemonic political projects can be confronted.[75]

Chantal Mouffe's conception of an agonistic public sphere also takes seriously the idea that private interests cannot – and should not – be bracketed in deliberative settings, and that differences in the social hierarchy continue to exist even when individuals reason together in institutional arrangements aiming for non-coercive communication. Privilege exists, and procedures and regulations are not always able to neutralise power differences (being addressed here is Jürgen Habermas's notions of deliberative democracy and the ideal speech situation).

Three critical points against liberal/deliberative citizenship theories can be extracted from agonal citizenship theory: *first*, its proponents' allegedly narrow cognitive/rational focus that ignores the importance of emotions and passions in politics; *second*, their political ontology where individuals are the primary political unit; and *third*, their attempt to eradicate conflict to reach consensus. As pointed out by one of Mouffe's foremost interpreters in the philosophy of education, Claudia Ruitenberg, "political education cannot consist in skills of reasoning and civic virtues alone, but must also take into account the desire for belonging to collectivities, and attendant political emotions."[76]

The aim of agonal democracy theory is a vital, vibrant public sphere where existing conflicts and political passions are not ignored or eradicated but rather channelled and sublimated, accompanied by an education that fosters the capacity to act as political adversaries rather than enemies. Importantly, then, the goal is not conflict but to avoid the kind of repression of emotions that leads to even more conflict.

Both agonal and liberal theories of democracy and citizenship aim to be accommodating and inclusive. Accepting for a fact that politics is about configuring we/them distinctions and acknowledging the existence of passions in the political field, agonal theory may come across as less exclusive than approaches that emphasise cognitivist-rational argumentation.[77] However, despite proponents' insistence on the opposite, the theory remains vulnerable to charges of being rigged for conflict between groups (identity politics). It could also be held that liberal and agonal citizenship theories form a polarity – oriented around the notion of competing life-views – where each is feeding itself by critiquing the other and both with good points.

Citizenship and (More) Politics

As we have seen, the tensions in the concept of democracy, identified by Rosanvallon as the coexistence of "the good and the vague" are also reflected in theories of citizenship education and how they relate to the political dimension(s). Some theories focus mostly on the students in terms of their identity, subjectivity, life-views, and so forth, while others are more concerned with the curriculum and who should decide over it. The more didactical literature typically focuses on factors like critical thinking skills, classroom discussions, deliberation, and so forth. However, a matter of less prominence are questions about the aims/purposes of education as society's 'ground-power' extending to asking what *kind* of society education should realise.

As we have seen, a central dimension in both liberal and agonal citizenship is the question about *who*: Who should be heard, included, have influence or decide over education? These questions, while relevant for education, do not fully capture the *political* dimension of education in a democracy. I would argue that although it is natural that education has a focus on identity and subjectivity, a too narrow focus on the who-question – us, them, inclusion, exclusion – seems to miss a common, political dimension that is much needed in a time of planetary crisis when the economic and political arrangements of the instituted order, such as patterns of production and big-tech capitalism, ought to be under attack from all of us.[78] As we shall see shortly, another problem with emphasising the who-question and questions about identity is that much contemporary populism feeds on this narrative.

In a discussion about ontology and the who-question in democratic theory, Andrew Dobson turns to Jane Bennett's question of what constitutes the political. The background for Dobson/Bennett is the discussion about who should be counted and who has the right to be heard in democratic deliberations. Do, for example, animals, children, future generations or ecosystems count as relevant parties? Do they have agency; do they have rights? According to Dobson, such discussions are unproductive since they are impossible to determine. Instead of posing the who-question and asking for relevant criteria for subject- or agent-hood, he proposes to turn the question around to ask *what constitutes the political*. The answer, with reference to Jane Bennett, is that *the political is constituted when a public coalesce around a problem*.

This reconceptualisation moves the focus from the 'who' of democracy (who counts as the demos) to the *what*, that is, to the proper field of politics. It thus helps sort out the conflation of subjectivity and the political that we find in (for example) Gert Biesta. A further advantage is that it enables us to think about politics, also democratic politics, in a larger setting – the world or the planet – without having to dive into endless discussions about anthropocentrism, dualism (subject/object, human/nonhuman), and so forth. The common ground can thus be set on political terms: institutions and that which lies between us, with all that entails.

More generally speaking, educational thought has been inclined, especially under neoliberalism, to downplay the *political*, instituting dimensions of democracy. This happens in many different ways. Making the *individual into the primary unit* (ontological and political individualism) whereby subjects understand themselves as responsible for managing their lives and their families is a decisive step in this direction. A second step, tied especially to the educational system, is to *frame education as competition*. The ideal of meritocracy, when combined with hopes of succeeding/advancing inside a hierarchical system, sets the horizon of individuals inside a presentist, hamster-wheel type of society.[79]

An adequate term used by critics to describe the "the affective mechanisms of the neoliberal rationality" is *cruel optimism*. The pursuit of social mobility, job security, equality and well-being, which "gives the individual a sense of purpose and meaning in life," has a downside, Mario Di Paolantonio notes: "Because these objects remain unattainable to most, their pursuit merely engages the individual in a constant struggle of self-management and self-improvement that ultimately keeps her from engaging in collective political action."[80] The cruel optimism of self-management and self-improvement in schools and universities thus "ends up usurping what is educational in education."[81] With individual subjects pitted against each other in an unending race, the liberating potential of democratic education becomes drowned in notions of individual opportunity – equal opportunity, upward mobility, educational rights – while purposes that can only meaningfully be conceptualised as collective interests, the concerns of citizens, never reach the public screen.

A third step to depoliticisation is to *reduce political concerns to questions of social integration*. Much of the international literature on citizenship education, including policy documents, strongly associates democracy with social integration related to non-political bodies such as work, church, community life, and so forth.[82] This notion of citizenship education reduces democracy to a vision of peaceful coexistence with our differences.[83] As Leonel Pérez Expósito asserts, this replacement of theoretically well-grounded categories for political participation with "less controversial categories, such as civic engagement, which are also theoretically less clear and well grounded" leads to "a demotion of the political."[84] Similarly, a study of European classrooms finds a "strong, perhaps dominant tradition that fails to discriminate between education for democracy related to the government and democracy related to other social institutions such as work life, church, local community and so forth."[85] Teachers in France and the UK use vague definitions of democracy such as "living in society" or simply "living together," and as political scientist Kjetil Börhaug observes, these definitions serve to "minimise teaching about political life, and instead focus on how to live together in class and at school in a respectful, tolerant way."[86] Indeed, the studies of Péres Expósito and Börhaug identify a strong tendency in educational thought and practice to *depoliticise the notion of democracy*. The most obvious cases include when we forget that democracy is a form of government and not only arrangements for living together in plurality, and when political categories such as class – a position in the social hierarchy – are displaced by cultural categories such as life-views.

At the deeper level of significations, depoliticisation takes place when political action is seen as futile, without real impact or irrelevant. This may be the case when the theories we use to analyse democracy (and education) *mirror the status quo* so that the relationship and potential differences between the instituted and the instituting society is occulted. In short, a properly political perspective needs to consider society as a whole, to identify power structures and place responsibility where it belongs: with those who are in the position to decide and influence others. If a theory loses sight of socio-political perspectives, focusing only on individuals and their interrelations, there is a clear drift toward depoliticisation.

How Populism Destroys the Idea of Education Proper

This chapter started with Aristotle's dictum that the prime duty of a lawgiver is to provide for the education of the young, and that every regime has a corresponding notion of (character) education. We have also seen how John

Dewey argues that a democracy – which for him is a regime aimed at self-improvement – has more reason to take interest in education for all its members than other kinds of regimes. Endorsing both these beliefs, I have also argued that the concept of education can function as a self-stabilising norm for a society that institutes itself explicitly. By explicitly questioning education's purpose and contents, such a society establishes its own understanding of what a worthwhile education might mean. This, I believe, is the essence of the social instituting process that Castoriadis calls the "project of autonomy."

In earlier chapters, I have also argued that even totalitarian societies pay close attention to their educational systems: not in order to produce autonomous, reflexive subjects, but in order to prevent their emergence. However, I would argue, there are also regimes in existence that do not value education in any of these forms, but rather thrive on discrediting the value of education and knowledge. I am thinking here about the peculiar logic of populism, especially right-wing populism.

In an increasingly polarised world with neoliberal oligarchy on the one hand and a weakened demos (Brown) on the other, the political field is frequently being roused by populist movements that, if they gain access to power, soon start to set limits to democratic procedures and processes.[87] Across the industrialised world, in nation after nation, traditional parties and politicians are replaced by ad-hoc parties that are more like movements, headed by leaders who often have no political experience whatsoever, which is exactly why they can present themselves as the true representatives of the people. In cascades of anti-political and populist movements from left to right, the current order is attacked for its failure to represent the people. In short – and sometimes for very good reasons – the legitimacy of the established political order is rapidly dwindling.

Populism can be seen as a protest against a range of tendencies in late modernity, such as growing inequalities, meritocracy with its winner-take-all ethos and other social injustices. The term itself holds different meanings; here I shall use it to refer to a mode of approaching, framing and addressing political issues that affects how we see and value institutions such as education, especially democratic education.[88]

Contemporary populist discourse rejects a society controlled by elites. This rejection is based on the belief that ordinary people are fully capable of forming their own opinions and political views without being instructed by experts. Populism embraces this essentially democratic belief but often disregards deliberative principles, for example, that democracy, in order to function, needs education and a public sphere where opinions are tested and refined, politically and intersubjectively.

The core of a populist scenario, then, is the opposition between the people and one or several elites, where most parties and positions of power are dominated by the latter. This analysis is basically sound – especially in times like these, when oligarchs, clans and corporations are in control of important institutions. What is more problematic in populism is how it conceives the relationship between the people and their (often self-appointed) spokespersons: the populist leaders. Indeed, the core of populism, as I see it, is its practice of leadership. For people are not the populists – their leaders are.

A comparison with direct democracy can be useful here. In contrast to direct democracy, where the people set the political agenda, the (typically right-wing) populist talks *to* the people through *appeals*: typically appealing to their discontent, resentment and desire for recognition or influence. Right-wing populism is not a social movement from below, from the people, but a movement built around a leader who claims to be the people's only true representative.[89] In practice, these populists typically build their position by attracting attention with more or less outrageous claims, changing positions frequently and blaming others, sometimes with humour and ambiguity. In contrast to classical political deliberation, then, most populist leaders are unembarrassed by inconsistent or weak argumentation, and they are often emotional, especially when addressing feelings of being excluded or marginalised. They even include themselves among the marginalised, as real estate magnate and multimillionaire Donald Trump did on many occasions. His attempt to overturn the presidential election in Washington in January 2021 is the most blatant outburst of this perverted logic – but we do not need to look to the United States for examples – also seemingly well-functioning democracies, like Norway's, have their populist factions.

In the years 2013 to 2021, Norway had a liberal-conservative government where the second largest party was the populist Progress Party. In the early months of 2020, the Minister of Justice, Tor Mikkel Wara, from this party, publicly taunted the Norwegian Police Security Service for taking care of his personal safety. The reason for heightened security around his person was a series of attacks against his property that had actually, as it turned out later, been staged by Wara's own partner, Laila Bertheussen, in order to frame a leftist, political theatre group. The police, powerless to defend themselves, were only doing their work. Another person from the same party, Anders Anundsen, was appointed Minister of Justice in the same government. A few years before, he had publicly – accompanied by the press – burned his local newspaper in disagreement with its editorial profile. A third Minister of Justice from the Progress Party, Sylvi Listhaug, left her position after an infamous Facebook post where she accused the social-democratic opposition (the Norwegian Labour Party) of caring more about terrorists than national security.[90]

Taunting the police (Wara), burning newspapers as a public statement (Anundsen) and publishing unreasonable claims (Listhaug) are all acts that undermine respect for public and legal institutions, draining the public sphere of reasonable argumentation. The remarkable fact, of course, is that these acts were performed by sitting (or with Anundsen, upcoming) Ministers of Justice, Public Security and Immigration (2013–2018). But from a populist background – having built their power base on resentment – it makes 'sense' to be against the establishment even though one is appointed to administer it.

Populist ideology claims that people – ordinary people – can make sensible choices without interference or guidance. This seems fair in many ways. But an important concern for a political democracy is not just to express *all* kinds of viewpoints, but in addition to care about how these viewpoints have been shaped, for example, whether they have been deliberated through collective, participatory processes or whether they have emerged in political (one-way) rallies. There is a huge difference between processes where different viewpoints are deliberated following argumentative procedures, and the way expressions of prejudice, resentment and fear are cultivated in so-called echo chambers. However, according to populist logic, to insist on distinctions of this kind is just another example of the logic of the *elites*.[91] Populist leaders claim that people should be free to mean whatever they mean, without being asked what their opinions are based on and whether they are reasonable in a *larger* perspective. Society as a whole is *not* what these leaders are after – but rather the opposite, to cultivate their own partisan group in opposition to all others.

The rise of right-wing populism is a direct threat to democratic education. I say this because the populist framework, in keeping with its anti-elitism, does not accept that education or knowledge should play any special role in the formation of political opinions. From a populist point of view, the question of validity is not only irrelevant, but almost meaningless, including distinctions between a well-founded and unfounded argument, second order evaluations and the question of what kinds of education – on which grounds – are considered formative, valuable and desirable. In other words, populism does not recognise that democratic *paideia* legitimises the principle of majority rule (Castoriadis). On the contrary, populism thrives by ignoring and denying the value of the distinction between what is important and unimportant, significant and insignificant, justified and unjustified. Based on the premise that people can define their own interests – albeit paradoxically, voiced by their leader-representative – its focus is on individual *rights* rather than collective, democratic politics and *interests*. This is where many nations find themselves today: needing a vocabulary for voicing collective concerns but with few theoretical resources to do so. In the next and final chapter, I turn to this question and try to outline some perspectives for the future.

Notes

1. I use the term 'regime' rather than 'government' in order to include ways of living and acting politically beyond the elected government apparatus.
2. Aristotle, *The Politics*, book VIII, i. 1337a11, trans. T. A. Sinclair, revised and re-presented by Trevor J. Saunders (Penguin Classics, 1981).
3. Castoriadis, "Power, Politics, Autonomy," 145.
4. Castoriadis, "Power, Politics, Autonomy," 145–46.
5. Paideia is the Greek concept of bildung.
6. Brown, *Undoing the Demos*, 175.
7. Brown, *Undoing the Demos*, 177.
8. Cornelius Castoriadis, "Democracy as Procedure and Democracy as a Regime," *Constellations* 4, no. 1 (1997): 11.
9. For Habermas, democratic legitimacy is produced pragmatically, through legitimate procedures.
10. Brown, *Undoing the Demos*, 178–79.
11. *The Guardian*, https://www.theguardian.com/world/2021/jul/15/kremlin-papers-appear-to-show-putins-plot-to-put-trump-in-white-house
12. Pierre Rosanvallon, "The Political Theory of Democracy," in *Pierre Rosanvallon's Political Thought*, ed. Oliver Flügel-Martinsen, Franziska Martinsen, Stephen W. Sawyer and Daniel Schulz (Bielefeld: Bielefeld University Press, transcript, 2018), 27.
13. Rosanvallon, "The Political Theory of Democracy," 27.
14. Rosanvallon, "The Political Theory of Democracy," 27.
15. French revolutionaries never considered the new constitution as democratic, and according to Rosanvallon (25) the word 'democracy' was never referred to during the debates in France over the right to vote between 1789 and 1791. Similarly, during the American Revolution, the word 'democracy' was used only in a negative sense. 'Republican' was the preferred term, building on the Roman tradition.
16. Representation was never a principle in ancient Greek democracy.
17. V-Dem, https://www.v-dem.net/en/. In political theory, the relationships between many of these variables are subject to discussion, not least concerning the question of how much equality is needed for a democracy to be real, to work according to its own principles, and whether there is a zero-sum game between equality (or security) and freedom. This discussion that took place especially between liberals and republicans around the turn of the century returns from time to time, and underlies

some of our discussions, but will not be the focus here. Instead I accept that the variables are important and can be weighted and related in different ways. But as already announced, people's self-rule (not institutional arrangements and classification of democracy in terms of questions about, rights, identity, etc.) is the main guide in the following.

18. V-Dem, 2021.

19. Vebjörn Nordhagen, *Social Inequality and Political Disengagement: Social Class and the Sense of Entitlement to Have an Opinion* (Master thesis in sociology, Dept. of Sociology and Human Geography, University of Oslo, 2019).

20. See, e.g., Jens Brun, "Civic and Citizenship Education in Denmark."

21. Following the Persian wars, with great military sacrifices, peasants demanded compensation and a share in politics.

22. Mogens Herman Hansen, "The Tradition of Ancient Greek Democracy and Its Importance for Modern Democracy. Historisk-filosofiske meddelelser 93" (Copenhagen: The Royal Danish Academy of Science and Letters, 2005); Josiah Ober, *The Athenian Revolution: Essays on Ancient Greek Democracy and Political Theory* (Princeton, NJ: Princeton University Press, 1996).

23. Castoriadis, "The Greek *Polis*," 113.

24. Castoriadis, "The Greek *Polis*," 113

25. Castoriadis, "The Greek *Polis*," 113.

26. Mogens Herman Hansen, *The Athenian Democracy in the Age of Demosthenes: Structure, Principles, and Ideology* (Oxford: Blackwell, 1991); Hansen, "The Tradition of Ancient Greek Democracy."

27. Kurt A. Raaflaub, Robert W. Wallace and Josiah Ober, *Origins of Democracy in Ancient Greece*. The Joan Palevsky Imprint in Classical Literature (Berkeley: University of California Press, 2007), 5. Other important arrangements were the many cultural and religious festivals, games, and the annual tragedy competitions.

28. Ober, *The Athenian Revolution*.

29. Hansen, *The Athenian Democracy in the Age of Demosthenes*.

30. This critique is timely. Nonetheless, contemporary critics who insist that the first democracy was undemocratic due to the exclusion of women and slaves might like to consider how inclusive other regimes at the time were in comparison, and also to recall that women's suffrage in modern democracies is still only around 100 years old.

31. The term 'self-stabilising norms' comes from Reinhart Koselleck, *The Practice of Conceptual History: Timing History, Spacing Concepts* (Stanford, CA: Stanford University Press, 2002).

32. This line of reasoning is developed in Straume, "Bildung from Paideia to the Modern Subject" and in Straume, *Danningens filosofihistorie*.

33. This argument is developed more fully in Straume, *Danningens filosofihistorie*.

34. Castoriadis, "The Greek *Polis*."

35. See Arendt, *The Human Condition*. The private affairs of the household included, for Arendt, questions of necessity such as economy. She went very far

– further than Castoriadis – in theorising the public sphere as a space reserved for freedom, where citizens could become visible for each other as unique individuals, through action and speech.

36. Castoriadis, "Power, Politics, Autonomy," 159.

37. Castoriadis, "The Imaginary," 12.

38. Mark Sagoff, *The Economy of the Earth: Philosophy, Law, and the Environment* (Cambridge: Cambridge University Press, 1988), 53.

39. Sagoff, *The Economy of the Earth*, 52–53.

40. Charles Taylor, *Human Agency and Language: Philosophical Papers I* (Cambridge: Cambridge University Press, 1985).

41. Marianna Papastephanou, "Genocide, Diversity and John Dewey's Progressive Education," *Metaphilosophy* 47, nos. 4–5 (October 2016).

42. http://www.jaas.gr.jp/jjas/PDF/2007/No.18-107.pdf

43. Dewey, *Democracy and Education*, 86.

44. Or as he says, two elements in one criterion.

45. Dewey, *Democracy and Education*, 86–87.

46. Dewey, *Democracy and Education*, 87.

47. Dewey, *Democracy and Education*, 87.

48. Dewey, *Democracy and Education*, 87.

49. Dewey, *John Dewey: The Later Works 1925–1954*, vol. 14, electronic version.

50. According to Pierre Rosanvallon, Dewey's identification of democracy with society rather than the affairs of the state echoes the older tradition, voiced by Alexis de Toqueville (author of *Democracy in America*) when democracy was still described as a social/sociological ideal of equality and not a name for the existing political regime. Pierre Rosanvallon, "The Political Theory of Democracy," in *Pierre Rosanvallon's Political Thought*, ed. Oliver Flügel-Martinsen et al. (Bielefeld: Bielefeld University Press, 2019), 25

51. Rosanvallon, "The Political Theory of Democracy," 25.

52. Dewey, *John Dewey: The Later Works 1925–1954*, vol. 14, electronic edition.

53. Numerous articles on Dewey are being published each year.

54. Wilfred Carr and Anthony Hartnet, *Education and the Struggle for Democracy: The Politics of Educational Ideas* (Buckingham: Open University Press, 1996), 65.

55. This category is an oversimplification where different thinkers are grouped together by me.

56. Amy Gutmann, *Democratic Education: With a New Preface and Epilogue*, rev. ed. (Princeton, NJ: Princeton University Press, 1999), xi. *Democratic Education* was first published in 1987 and republished with a new preface and epilogue in 1999.

57. Gutmann, *Democratic Education*, 16.

58. John Rawls, *Political Liberalism*, expanded ed. (New York: Columbia University Press, 2005). 'Public' and 'political' are more or less synonyms for Rawls.

59. Rawls, *Political Liberalism*, 3–4.

60. Rawls, *Political Liberalism*, 4.

61. In recent years, under the presidency of Donald J. Trump, the US has been tested hard in this respect.

62. Wolin, *Politics and Vision*, 536.

63. Gutmann, *Democratic Education*, 14.

64. Gutmann, *Democratic Education*, 14.

65. Gutmann, *Democratic Education*, 46.

66. Like other works by Gutmann: *The Spirit of Compromise: Why Governing Demands It and Campaigning Undermines It*, with Dennis Thompson (Princeton, NJ: Princeton University Press, 2012); *Why Deliberative Democracy?*, with Dennis Thompson (Princeton, NJ: Princeton University Press, 2004).

67. See, e.g., Marianna Papastephanou, "Philosophical Presuppositions of Citizenship Education and Political Liberalism," in *The SAGE Handbook of Education for Citizenship and Democracy* (London: SAGE, 2008). Papastephanou concludes that "the Rawlsian conception of education would produce an institutional apparatus for the perpetuation of inequality, unconscious of its role in social reproduction [. . .] So the educational dilemma is either to cling to liberalism or to contribute to its reformulation."

68. "What is taught about climate change to students in the nation's public schools" is a matter of conflict "before state boards of education, in local school districts and individual schools, and even within the minds of science teachers" (Branch 2019 https://www.aft.org/ae/winter2019-2020/branch).

69. George Packer, *Last Best Hope: America in Crisis and Renewal* (New York: Farrar, Straus and Giroux, 2021).

70. Schwartz, Sarah. "Map: Where Critical Race Theory Is Under Attack (2021, June 11). Education Week. Retrieved February 23 2023 from http://www.edweek.org/leadership/map-where-critical-race-theory-is-under-attack/2021/06.

71. Mouffe, *The Return of the Political*.

72. The latter is a definite departure from Schmitt, who argued that there could be no friend/enemy distinction within a democratic polity, and hence no pluralist version of democracy. Chantal Mouffe, *On the Political. Thinking in Action* (London: Routledge, 2005), 19.

73. Mouffe, *On the Political*; Claudia W. Ruitenberg, "Educating Political Adversaries: Chantal Mouffe and Radical Democratic Citizenship Education," *Studies in Philosophy and Education* 28, no. 3 (2008).

74. Mouffe, *On the Political*, 3.

75. Ruitenberg, "Educating Political Adversaries," 274.

76. Claudia Ruitenberg calls the latter practices "masculine," which is not meant as a compliment.

77. The question about identity politics is a complicated one. One the one hand, when concepts and categories from the cultural disciplines – identity, religion, etc. – are given political centre stage, it becomes harder to articulate concerns about economic arrangements, injustice and planetary survival, and questions of class, economy, etc., tend to fall out of sight. On the other hand, these questions are among

the most politicised in Western democracies and even a matter of life and death in many cases.

78. Katariina Tiainen et al., "Democratic Education for Hope: Contesting the Neoliberal Common Sense," *Studies in Philosophy and Education* 38, no. 6 (2019). See also Paolantonio, "The Cruel Optimism of Education."

79. Tiainen et al., "Democratic Education for Hope," 642.

80. Paolantonio, "The Cruel Optimism of Education," 148–49.

81. Kjetil Børhaug, "Ein skule for demokratiet?," *Norsk pedagogisk tidsskrift* 88 nos. 2–3 (2004); Kjetil Børhaug, "Voter Education – the Political Education of Norwegian Lower Secondary Schools," *Utbildning och Demokrati* 14, no. 3 (2005).

82. Biesta, *Learning Democracy*; Børhaug, "Ein skule for demokratiet?"; Leonel Pérez Expósito, "Rethinking Political Participation: A Pedagogical Approach for Citizenship Education," *Theory and Research in Education* 12, no. 2 (2014); Straume, "'Learning' and Signification."

83. Expósito, "Rethinking Political Participation," 230.

84. Börhaug, "Ein skule for demokratiet?," 207.

85. Börhaug, "Voter Education," 55.

86. Andrew Arato, "Socialism and Populism," *Constellations* 26, no. 3 (2019): 469; see also Jean L. Cohen, "What's Wrong with the Normative Theory (and the Actual Practice) of Left Populism," *Constellations* 26, no. 3 (2019).

87. I have left out most forms of left-wing populism such as the Latin-American examples and the populism described especially by Ernesto Laclau, which is a strategy for establishing hegemony.

88. Arato, "Socialism and Populism"; Nadia Urbinati, *Me the People: How Populism Transforms Democracy* (Cambridge, MA: Harvard University Press, 2019).

89. This allegation was particularly vile since the same party's youth camp had suffered a large massacre in 2011.

90. For populists, academics are definitely an elite.

CHAPTER FIVE

∾

Extraordinary Politics, Extraordinary Education

How Does a Society Change?

Let me start this chapter with a few statements to sum up some of the ideas we have visited so far. First of all, how do societies change? They change (on a deeper level) by changing their social imaginaries. This change is not acted out by individuals, but takes place at the collective or social level, openly or implicitly. Where do new imaginaries come from? Or more concretely, how can they be called forth? One answer is that new imaginaries, and altered meaning of existing ones, emerge in the in-betweens where different imaginary significations meet, collide or, more frequently, coexist in tension. In other words, directing attention to the differences between the instituted imaginary and society's capacity for self-institution is an intellectual task for a society that wishes to govern and change itself. If this is more or less right, then elucidation of these tensions, debating how to act upon them in politics and education, can represent a reflexive, social-historical (as opposed to individualist) approach to societal change.

On this basis, it is not a trivial incident when education is deprived of its political significance. When, for example, education is conceptualised as linear techniques for learning in order to produce test scores in the most efficient ways, we lose sight of self-reflexive questions related to various forms of socio-political *meaning*. A society that ignores these socio-political questions is a depoliticised society. Neoliberalism – ideologically masking itself as non-ideology in the form of quasi-markets – has driven this depoliticisation to an art. For the 'learning' paths of modern individualism, increasingly fuelled by big tech, never lead into the deeper kinds of questioning that –

119

luckily – every young person will naturally be drawn toward. To extinguish our innate impulse to question the state of things requires a long process of consumerist grooming.

Despite all its flux, then, neoliberalism is the perfect ideology for the peculiar status quo that characterises capitalism, where there is acceleration but no real, societal change. Its restricted imaginaries (individualisation, reductionism, instrumentalism, occultation of collectivity and false notions of freedom) is the true face of depoliticisation.

A massive transformation of minds, of social relations and political constellations is currently taking place across the world. Young minds are being mapped from an early age and tracked, targeted and manipulated through clever uses of various emotional triggers such as brightly coloured lights, games, characters, jingles, role models who are actually salespeople, and probably a range of other mechanisms that we ordinary people are unaware of. The child's world of imagination and play is no longer a private place, but increasingly shaped by schooling where children are spoken of as young learners, but with technologies using children variously as investments, raw material, capital and consumers. As big tech is penetrating our lifeworlds, these different subject positions and the domains they represent are increasingly entangled, muddled and difficult to recognise.

Education cannot solve, but nor can it stay unaffected by these sociopolitical problems. Behaviour surveillance and modification are of a scale which the schools' response, such as 'critical thinking skills,' can nowhere match. What we are witnessing here is a commercial appropriation of minds, but mixed with elements of warfare. For if war today implies weakening another regime, the best way of doing so would probably be to target and weaken the minds of those inhabitants, for example by eradicating the difference between truth and lies – much as Putin's Russia attempted in the US under Donald Trump's presidency. Putin's agenda, shared by Trump's former advisor Steve Bannon, was to exploit the weak points of democracies and ridicule them by creating distrust within the citizenry.[1] And indeed, at least until the outbreak of the war against Ukraine in February 2022, distrust in existing forms of democracy has been amounting. Many nominal democracies have experienced declining psychological investment – trust and belief – in democratic politics and a general political passivity (some call it 'apathy') especially among younger groups.

Numerous surveys conducted before the Russian invasion of Ukraine found that many young people did not see any real danger in the decline of Western democracies. But these trends were never total, because in certain affairs such as environmental protection and climate change, the interest in politics among young people has been strong and rising. Many young people across the world want to be counted as political subjects and demand to learn how to engage in politics.[2]

The Fridays for Future movement, inspired by the young Swedish activist Greta Thunberg, was a particularly potent global movement of young people demanding, among other things, that their education become politically relevant. Fridays for Future and Plant-for-the-Planet – another movement started by a child – also demanded that adults act *responsibly*. In doing so, these movements appeared in a political arena, setting new initiatives in motion and demanding to be seen and heard – all central characteristics of what Hannah Arendt called *action*, the properly political mode of human activity.[3] However, Arendt was also very insistent in stating that children should be spared from taking such a position since, precisely, responsibility in political and worldly matters belongs to adults. She was strongly opposed to engaging children in politics and argued that schools should be non-political (in the sense of nonpartisan). However, and in a certain sense in Arendt's spirit, these children are charging adults with failing in *their* responsibility. In a remarkably clear and weighty speech to the 2018 United Nations Climate Change Conference (COP24) in Katowice, Poland, Greta Thunberg declared:

> My name is Greta Thunberg. I am 15 years old. I am from Sweden. I speak on behalf of Climate Justice Now. Many people say that Sweden is just a small country and it doesn't matter what we do. But I've learned you are never too small to make a difference. And if a few children can get headlines all over the world just by not going to school, then imagine what we could all do together if we really wanted to.
>
> But to do that, we have to speak clearly, no matter how uncomfortable that may be. You only speak of green eternal economic growth because you are too scared of being unpopular. You only talk about moving forward with the same bad ideas that got us into this mess, even when the only sensible thing to do is pull the emergency brake. You are not mature enough to tell it like it is. Even that burden you leave to us children. But I don't care about being popular. I care about climate justice and the living planet. Our civilization is being sacrificed for the opportunity of a very small number of people to continue making enormous amounts of money. Our biosphere is being sacrificed so that rich people in countries like mine can live in luxury. It is the sufferings of the many which pay for the luxuries of the few.[4]

As Thunberg's speech demonstrates, young activists' sense of impending and unfolding crises leads into a quest for politicisation that is out of the ordinary. When children are charging adults with failing their responsibility, they claim a political position on behalf of the future that is hitherto unheard of in political affairs. Like in classical Athenian democracy, they invoke *isegoria* and *parrhesia*, the right to speak truth to power. We could call it a claim of the extraordinary,[5] where the world needs to be "set aright," as Arendt said.

From One Crisis to the Next

Over the past decades, the world has been subjected to a series of global crises, moving from one crisis to the next. From a Nordic viewpoint, the narrative looks something like this, in the reverse: in February 2022, Russia invaded Ukraine with the intention of annihilating it as a nation. This event changed the geopolitical landscape in Europe and overshadowed everything that had happened so far in this decade, including the global COVID-19 pandemic (in Norwegian media, called the 'corona crisis') that had dominated the early 2020s. The pandemic came on top of, and eclipsed, what at that time was called the "most pressing crisis of our time," namely, the climate crisis and loss of species (the sixth mass extinction), as well as the crisis of the earth's biosystem (the planetary crisis). Together these elements can be reported as a *global eco-crisis*. This was the direct background for the school strikes (2016–2019, peaking in 2018) and the reason why, in Katowice, Greta Thunberg asked the world leaders to start treating the crisis as a crisis. Directly before, in 2015–2016, Europe experienced what was termed a *refugee or migration crisis*, where 1.3 million asylum seekers migrated from Syria, Afghanistan and African countries (notably Nigeria and Eritrea) and started marching north, from one nation to the next, being blocked at various points. Many are still stranded in camps, and many, many have drowned and are still drowning in the Mediterranean Sea. The refugee crisis was brought on by the war in Syria, following the Arab Spring, which in turn was fuelled, among other things, by the *global economic crisis* from 2007/2008, with the associated bank crisis affecting currency and finance. Before this, we had the so-called *war on terror* following the attack on the US's central institutions in September 2001, which involved many nations, accompanied by a large war industry and investors specialising in regions hit by disaster.[6]

On a more general level, globalisation and neoliberal reforms have undermined (some, not all) public institutions, environments and livelihoods in large parts of the world since the 1980s. Over the same period, many nations have become more polarised, with rising inequalities and a shifting political landscape. Among the most striking trends in my own country, Norway, is how statements that were considered extreme a few years ago have been uttered so frequently that they have moved the baseline for normal public debate. One might even say that the extreme defines the public agenda today, along with the long chain of perceived crises.

A child born in Norway in the year 2008 will thus have lived through a permanent chain of crises. N-gram searches in the Norwegian national library (English-language books and Norwegian newspapers) reveal that the first peak of the term 'crisis/crises' was in the early 1930s, when the global economic recession was unleashed after the collapse of the stock exchange. Another peak was in 1946, following the Second World War. But the real escalation of the term 'crisis/crises' started in the 1950s (English books) and 1960s (Norwegian newspapers), never returning to the level of the 1930s. The rising graph still contains peaks such as the year 1974, with the global oil crisis, but since the 1960s, the world seems to have gone from one crisis to the next, with ever-shortening intervals between each peak. A permanent sense of crisis is becoming the new norm, if we believe books and the public media. All these chained crises bring with them general and specific fears: fear of terrorists, fear of immigrants, fear of economic breakdown with loss of livelihood, fear of virus infections, fear of the generalised other (the Americans, the Russians, the Chinese, the Muslim), and fear of many natural phenomena.

The constant portrayal of crisis is a condition that seriously affects education, and the (admittedly bourgeois) ideal of a sheltered childhood from the nineteenth and early twentieth centuries no longer seems like an option. One of the effects I see from living in a permanent state of crisis is disengagement where we cease to attach any real sense of importance to what passes on the news screen, while becoming prone to quickly forget and/or regress into the private sphere (which, as I have argued, is no longer so private). To address our current predicaments, then, a first step could be to define the proper level of scale.

Crises and Questions of Scale

All of these crises are real, but on different scales, including the representations of the world and our place in it. At the far end of the scale looms the concept of the Anthropocene, where humans have become a geological factor. The notion of 'world' in the Anthropocene is the earth system, where nine "planetary boundaries" define the limits for a "safe operating space for humanity."[7] If these boundaries are transgressed, as half of them currently are (irreversibly), human life on the planet becomes unsustainable. Inside this scenario, the relevant notion of subjectivity refers to existence at the level of the species. In other words, agency relates to questions of the extinction or survival of our species.[8]

A problem with applying the planetary scale and Anthropocene as an educational or political framework is that this grand scale makes us lose sight of institutions and how people are situated differently in the social hierarchy. Human beings are animals, yes, but the kind of animal that builds institutions, and inside these institutions we invest meaning, we socialise ourselves, we manipulate each other, and we bind ourselves to laws which we have created for our societies as a whole. All of this is lost under the scale of the Anthropocene, where each epoch lasts tens of thousands of years.

At the other end of the spectrum, we find the level of the individual, whose subject position is reinforced and highlighted in our neoliberal era. However, as I have argued, the neoliberal individual is exposed and subjected to forces that make them vulnerable and isolated. Digital and social media are driving subjects to be constantly performing, self-representing and competing for attention ('likes'). This is a competition where everybody loses.

What would an educational response be? For a start, educators should avoid practices that leave individuals exposed to and in competition with each other and instead, as Christian Laval and Francis Vergne argue, adhere to collective categories emphasising the *instituting* imaginary and the public sphere that connects us all. "Nothing is more serious for the future of education," they argue, "than the weakening of our capacity to think and act together."[9]

What neoliberalism has made us forget is that between the species level and the individual – levels where we are essentially powerless – lies the level of institutions, where collective practices and empowering forms of recognition can take place. Such are the precarious conditions for politics where questions can be addressed. As Arendt tells us, *power* comes into being where people come together in their plurality. A proper scale for educational theory in these extraordinary circumstances is therefore institutions and the significations that infuse them with meaning. Acknowledging Castoriadis's words that "whatever depends on us, is our responsibility," but not more, we can now identify the proper level of educational purpose from which an educational approach can be developed.

The Ordinary in the Extraordinary

It seems fair to conclude that traditional forms of 'citizenship education' where students learn about the political order and their roles as future citizens in a polity of representative bodies are based on yesterday's political reality. When subjected to scrutiny, the instituted norms and significations characterising neoliberal representations of the world and of social life are hardly the norms that most of us hold dear and would like to defend. No-where is this more apparent than in matters of the environment, where the de facto instituted consumer culture – based on the acceleration of new, fabricated 'demands' based in new deficiencies of the consumer subjects – is at odds with educational norms. To provide just one example, the Norwe-gian influencer Sophie Elise (at 24) provoked a wave of reactions when she pointed out her newly discovered flaw: the lack of hair behind her ears, visible from a certain angle with a certain hairstyle, for which she promoted the 'solution' of tattooing false hairs. A large number of Norwegian teenagers suddenly found out that they, too, had this newly invented 'flaw' that im-mediately needed fixing.

In *Democracy and the Politics of the Extraordinary*, political thinker Andreas Kalyvas discusses situations where the normal, political day-to-day business is suspended, giving way to what he calls "foundational moments." These political moments stretch beyond the legal framework and the "basic pro-cedural rules of regimes," including changes "unfolding at the realm of the symbolic, like the transformation of shared meanings, the radical reorienta-tion of collective and individual values, and the construction of new political identities."[10] This description seems to fit the contemporary situation, where one reason for turning to the category of the 'extraordinary' is the need to address young people's sense of ecological grief, depression and/or alienation in a world that is losing collective meaning. It seems important that espe-cially children and young people are heard when speaking truth to power, while on a deeper level, the need for a space to form free subjectivities is also urgently needed.

The appeals to education for solving the 'big questions of our time' is not new, as we saw with the reactions to Sputnik in chapter 1. Today, the challenges posed to educators are nothing less than the global need to stall anthropogenic climate change and species extinction. The favoured response from policymakers and universities has so far been to educate *change agents*. To be sure, technological and social innovations are extremely important for a more sustainable development. The problem with demanding that we all become change agents and entrepreneurs (without social security), however, is the massive overburdening of individual subjects and the occultation of the social.

But what if education should *not* be aimed at 'solving' the greatest questions of our time, with the risk of failure and depression? Considering the magnitude of these challenges, perhaps a more modest aim is more ap-propriate and, not least, realistic. It seems to me that a more empowering (read: hope-sustaining) approach would be to prevent the collapse of our institutions by renewing them and to defer deep divisions as far as possible. The extraordinary does not necessarily mean something spectacular, like inventing technologies that will fix the climate or planetary crises, but perhaps equally important, refusing to support the current unsustainable development.

One example of an extraordinary turn in educational literature is the Norwegian book *Action, takk!* (Action, please!) by Astrid Sinnes.[11] As an experienced researcher in sustainability and science education, Sinnes has gradually turned her focus from asking what schools can do to train and inspire students toward looking at how schools can learn from young, engaged individuals. *Action, takk!* has a plethora of case stories and interviews with young people who have started small, eco-friendly businesses, are active in NGOs or engaged in other initiatives to generate a fair, circular, zero-waste economy. By sharing these examples and exploring them in class, educators may identify examples of the 'tools' and ideas that young people are looking for and demand. Importantly, for Sinnes, knowledge, skills, and competences are not enough: young people also need to *experience* sustainability and opportunities to develop their capacity as change agents in turbulent times. The time has passed, she states, for asking *if* schools should engage in transforming current practices. The question we now need to ask is *how*. Although I am reluctant to claim that all young people should become change agents – a term resembling the neoliberal entrepreneur – Sinnes's collection of practical examples is also a window for emphasising a collective engagement with the social institution (Laval and Vergne). For experiences with sustainability are not available to individuals in constant competition with each other: they are communal experiences aiming at the common good.

Sinnes's context is Norway, where schoolteachers are relatively free to organise their teaching practices without being overruled by parents or religious groups. It is perhaps doubtful that public schools in nations with very different political traditions could implement this kind of approach without protests. However, *if* parents and teachers would identify some common enemies of education proper – such as big-tech corporations that are currently invading schools across the world – it could be the start of a renewal of *common* purpose. On the individual level, limiting the power of so-called social media is hard and for the few; but one might hope for regulations: laws to self-bind and limit the desiring part of the self, collectively and individually. In ultimate terms, if we acknowledge that collective self-binding is a prerequisite for freedom, fostering this capacity should be a priority for those who care for the future of our humanity and the planet.

In ultimate terms, if we acknowledge that collective self-binding is a prerequisite for freedom, fostering this capacity should be a priority for those who care for the future of our humanity and the planet.

Notes

1. It has become more difficult to focus on this type of slow-cooking regime destruction after Putin moved from chaos tactics to outright terror against Ukraine.

2. O'Brien, Karen, Elin Selboe, and Bronwyn M. Hayward. "Exploring Youth Activism on Climate Change: Dutiful, Disruptive, and Dangerous Dissent." *Ecology and Society* 23, no. 3 (2018): 42.

3. Arendt, *The Human Condition*.

4. Greta Thunberg, https://www.lifegate.com/greta-thunberg-speech-cop24

5. Kalyvas, *Democracy and the Politics of the Extraordinary*.

6. Klein, Naomi. *The Shock Doctrine: The Rise of Disaster Capitalism*. New York: Picador, 2007.

7. Stockholm Resilience Centre, https://www.stockholmresilience.org/research/planetary-boundaries.html, accessed 9 February 2023.

8. On this scale, it also becomes clear, to me at least, that humans have become too numerous on the planet.

9. Laval and Vergne, Éducation *Démocratique*, 219, my translation.

10. Kalyvas, *Democracy and the Politics of the Extraordinary*, 5.

11. *Action, takk!* (Oslo: Universitetsforlaget, 2020).

~

Afterword

Every time a child is born, new family relations are also brought into the world. Hannah Arendt spoke of 'natality' as a fact of life whereby new beginnings are constantly introduced into the existing, 'old' world. When people become parents, they are faced with existential and political questions such as: What do we wish to realise in the time to come; what is so worthwhile that we want our child to be shaped by and live for it; what do I *really* believe in; what are the things from my own heritage that I would like to make exist beyond myself when I am gone? Similar questions are pondered by teachers from preschools to universities. With responsibility for the education of the young comes responsibility for the world, just as Arendt said. This insight is as old as the idea of commonality itself.

In the society where politics as we know it was first instituted, the first citizens were deeply concerned, according to Castoriadis, with what they collectively wanted to realise:

> When I say that the Greeks are for us a germ, I mean, first, that they never stopped thinking about this question: What is it that the institution of society ought to achieve? And second, I mean that in the paradigmatic case, Athens, they gave this answer: the creation of human beings living with beauty, living with wisdom, and loving the common good.[1]

Loving the common good is almost exactly the opposite of today's individualistic ideology. It does not seem realistic, at this or any other point in history, that all the world's nations should come to agree on any common set of values or purpose. But living in hope for the future, acknowledging the predicament of planetary limits *and* valuing the project of autonomy does not seem too farfetched. The question is, will we – some of us – be able to join forces and invest enough energy to push back against those forces that want to own, weaken and manipulate our wills? Such are the big questions of our time, it seems to me.

Note

1. Castoriadis, "Power, Politics, Autonomy," 123.

References

Aaberge, Rolf, Christophe André, Anne Boschini, Lars Calmfors, Kristin Gunnars-son, Mikkel Hermansen, Audun Langørgen, Petter Lindgren, Causa Orsetta, Jon Pareliussen, P-O Robling, Jesper Roine, Jakob Egholt Søgaard et al., "Increasing Income Inequality in the Nordics," *Nordic Economic Policy Review 2018*, Nordic Council of Ministers. Available at http://norden.diva-portal.org/smash/record.jsf?pid=diva2%3A1198429&dswid=-2405

Amnå, Erik. "The Personal, the Professional, and the Political: An Intertwined Perspective on the IEA Civic Education Studies." In *Influences of the IEA Civic and Citizenship Education Studies: Practice, Policy, and Research Across Countries and Regions*. Edited by Barbara Malak-Minkiewicz and Judith Torney-Purta, 185–93. Cham: Springer International Publishing AG, 2021.

Angebauer, Niklas. "Property and Capital in the Person: Lockean and Neo-liberal Self-Ownership." *Constellations* 27, no. 1 (2020): 50–62. https://doi.org/10.1111/1467-8675.12424

Arato, Andrew. "Socialism and Populism." *Constellations* 26, no. 3 (2019): 464–74.

Apple, Michael. *Ideology and Curriculum*, third edition. New York: RoutledgeFalmer, 2004.

Arendt, Hannah. *The Origins of Totalitarianism*. New York: Schocken Books, 1951/2004.

Arendt, Hannah. *The Human Condition*. Chicago: University of Chicago Press, 1998.

Arendt, Hannah. "The Crisis in Education." In *Between Past and Future. Eight Exer-cises in Political Thought*. 170–93. New York: Penguin, 2006.

Aristotle. *The Politics*. Translated by T. A. Sinclair, revised and re-presented by Trevor J. Saunders. London: Penguin, 1981.

Aronova, Elena. "The Congress for Cultural Freedom, Minerva, and the Quest for Instituting 'Science Studies' in the Age of Cold War." *Minerva* (London) 50, no. 3 (2012): 307–37.

Barrow, Robin. "Schools of Thought in Philosophy of Education." In *The SAGE Handbook of Philosophy of Education*. Edited by Richard Bailey, Robin Barrow, David Carr and Christine McCarthy, 21–35. London: SAGE, 2010.

Baune, Tove Aarsnes. *Den Skal Tidlig Krøkes: Skolen i Historisk Perspektiv*, revised edition. Oslo: Cappelen Akademisk forlag, 2007.

Biesta, G. J. J. "How General Can Bildung Be? Reflections on the Future of a Modern Educational Ideal." In *Educating Humanity: Bildung in Postmodernity*. Edited by Lars Løvlie, Klaus Peter Mortensen and Sven Erik Nordenbro, 61–74. Oxford: Blackwell, 2003.

Biesta, Gert J. J. "Against Learning. Reclaiming a Language for Education in an Age of Learning." *Nordic Studies in Education* 24, no. 1 (2004): 70–82.

Biesta, Gert J. J. "Why 'What Works' Won't Work: Evidence-Based Practice and the Democratic Deficit in Educational Research." *Educational Theory* 57, no. 1 (2007): 1–22.

Biesta, G. J. J. *Good Education in an Age of Measurement: Ethics, Politics, Democracy.* Boulder, CO: Paradigm, 2010.

Biesta, Gert J. J. *Learning Democracy in School and Society: Education, Lifelong Learning, and the Politics of Citizenship.* Rotterdam: SensePublishers, 2011.

Biesta, Gert J. J., and Carl Anders Säfström. "A Manifesto for Education." *Policy Futures in Education* 9, no. 5 (2011): 540–47. https://journals.sagepub.com/doi/pdf/10.2304/pfie.2011.9.5.540

Biesta, Gert J. J. "Interrupting the Politics of Learning." *Power and Education* 5, no. 1 (2013): 4–15. https://doi.org/10.2304/power.2013.5.1.4

Biesta, Gert J. J. *The Beautiful Risk of Education.* Interventions: Education, Philosophy, and Culture. Boulder, CO: Paradigm, 2014.

Biesta, Gert J. J. "Freeing Teaching from Learning: Opening Up Existential Possibilities in Educational Relationships." *Studies in Philosophy and Education* 34, no. 3 (2014): 229–43.

Biesta, Gert J. J. *Obstinate Education: Reconnecting School and Society.* Leiden: Brill Sense, 2019.

Børhaug, Kjetil. "Ein skule for demokratiet?," *Norsk pedagogisk tidsskrift* 88, nos. 2–3 (2004): 205–19.

Børhaug, Kjetil. "Voter Education – the Political Education of Norwegian Lower Secondary Schools." *Utbildning och Demokrati* 14, no. 3 (2005): 51–73.

Bowers, C. A. *The Culture of Denial. Why the Environmental Movement Needs a Strategy for Reforming Universities and Public Schools.* New York: SUNY Press, 1997.

Branch, Glenn. "Science Teachers in the Hot Seat: Climate Change Education in a Polarized Society." American Federation of Teachers: *American Educator*, Winter 2019–2020. https://www.aft.org/ae/winter2019-2020/branch

Brock-Utne, Birgit. "Language of Instruction and Student Performance." *International Review of Education* 53, nos. 5/6 (2007): 509–30.

Brown, Wendy. *Undoing the Demos.* Cambridge, MA/London: Zone Books, 2015.

Brun, Jens. "Civic and Citizenship Education in Denmark 1999–2019: Discourses of Progressive and Productive Education." In *Influences of the IEA Civic and Citizenship Education Studies: Practice, Policy, and Research Across Countries and Regions.* Edited by Barbara Malak-Minkiewicz and Judith Torney-Purta, 49–62. Cham: Springer International Publishing AG, 2021. https://doi.org/10.1007/978-3-030-71102-3_5

Callan, Autonomy, *Encyclopedia of Educational Theory and Philosophy, Vol. 1.* Edited by D. C. Phillips, 69–72. London/Thousand Oaks, CA: SAGE, 2014.

Carr, Wilfred and Anthony Hartnett. *Education and the Struggle for Democracy: The Politics of Educational Ideas.* Buckingham: Open University Press, 1996.

Castoriadis, Cornelius. *The Imaginary Institution of Society.* Translated by Kathleen Blamey. Cambridge, MA: MIT Press, 1987.

Castoriadis, Cornelius. "The Greek Polis and the Creation of Democracy." In *Philosophy, Politics, Autonomy: Essays in Political Philosophy.* Edited and translated by David Ames Curtis, 81–123. New York/Oxford: Oxford University Press, 1991.

Castoriadis, Cornelius. "Power, Politics, Autonomy." In *Philosophy, Politics, Autonomy. Essays in Political Philosophy* 143–74. Edited and translated by David Ames Curtis. New York: Oxford University Press, 1991.

Castoriadis, Cornelius. "The Imaginary: Creation in the Social-Historical Domain." In *World in Fragments: Writings on Politics, Society, Psychoanalysis, and the Imagination.* Edited and translated by David Ames Curtis, 3–18. Stanford: Stanford University Press, 1997.

Castoriadis, Cornelius. "Democracy as Procedure and Democracy as a Regime." *Constellations* 4, no. 1 (1997): 1–18.

Castoriadis Cornelius, "Psychoanalysis and Politics." In *World in Fragments: Writings on Politics, Society, Psychoanalysis, and the Imagination.* Edited and translated by David Ames Curtis, 125–36. Stanford: Stanford University Press, 1997.

Castoriadis, Cornelius. "Psychoanalysis and Philosophy." In *The Castoriadis Reader.* Translated and edited by David Ames Curtis, 349–60. Oxford: Blackwell, 1997.

Castoriadis, Cornelius. "Done and to Be Done." In *The Castoriadis Reader.* Edited and translated by David Ames Curtis, 361–417. Oxford: Blackwell, 1997.

Castoriadis, Cornelius. "Psyche and Education." In *Figures of the Thinkable.* Translated by Helen Arnold, 165–87. Stanford CA: Stanford University Press, 2007.

Cohen, Jean L. "What's Wrong with the Normative Theory (and the Actual Practice) of Left Populism." *Constellations* 26, no. 3 (2019): 391–407.

Deem, Rosemary, Ka Ho Mok, and Lisa Lucas. "Transforming Higher Education in Whose Image?" *Higher Education Policy* 21, no. 1 (2008): 83–97.

Descombes, Vincent. "The Philosophy of Collective Representations." Translated by Anthony Cheal Pugh. *History of the Human Sciences* 13 no. 1 (2000): 37–49.

Dewey, John. *Democracy and Education.* New York: Simon & Schuster, 1916/1997.

Dewey, John. *John Dewey: The Later Works 1925–1954, Vol. 14*, electronic version.

Dobson, Andrew. *Listening for Democracy: Recognition, Representation, Reconciliation.* Oxford: Oxford University Press, 2014.

Doyle, Natalie. *Marcel Gauchet and the Loss of Common Purpose: Imaginary Islam and the Crisis of European Democracy.* Lanham, MD: Lexington Books, 2018.

Expósito, Leonel Pérez. "Rethinking Political Participation: A Pedagogical Approach for Citizenship Education." *Theory and Research in Education* 12, no. 2 (2014): 229–51.

Griffiths, Tom G., and Cardona, Euridice Charon. "Education for a Social Transformation: Soviet University Education Aid in the Cold War Capitalist World-System." *European Education* 47, no. 3 (2015): 226–41.

Guillemin, Elodie. "An Investigation of Education as Subjectification: Biesta's Use of Example." MA thesis in education. Faculty of Education, University of Oslo, 2022.

Gutmann, Amy. *Democratic Education: With a New Preface and Epilogue*, revised paperback edition. Princeton, NJ: Princeton University Press, 1999.

Hansen, Mogens Herman. *The Athenian Democracy in the Age of Demosthenes: Structure, Principles, and Ideology.* Norman, OK/Oxford: Blackwell, 1991.

Hansen, Mogens Herman. "The Tradition of Ancient Greek Democracy and Its Importance for Modern Democracy. Historisk-filosofiske meddelelser 93." Copenhagen: The Royal Danish Academy of Science and Letters, 2005.

Hänninen, Sakari, Kirsi-Marja Lehtelä and Paula Saikkonen (eds). *The Relational Nordic Welfare State: Between Utopia and Ideology.* London: Edward Elgar, 2019.

Honneth, Axel. *The Struggle for Recognition: The Moral Grammar of Social Conflicts.* Cambridge: Polity Press, 1995.

Honneth, Axel. "Grounding Recognition: A Rejoinder to Critical Questions," *Inquiry* 45, no. 4 (2002): 499–519. https://doi.org/10.1080/002017402320947577

Horlacher, Rebekka. *The Educated Subject and the German Concept of Bildung.* London: Routledge, 2016.

Humboldt, Wilhelm von, "Theory of Bildung." Translated by Gillian Horton-Krüger. In *Teaching as a Reflective Practice: The German Didaktik Tradition.* Edited by Ian Westbury, Stefan Hopmann and Kurt Riquarts, 57–61, Studies in Curriculum Theory. Mahwah, NJ: Lawrence Erlbaum Associates, 2012.

Kaiser, David. "The Physics of Spin: Sputnik Politics and American Physicists in the 1950s." *Social Research* 73, no. 4 (2006): 1225–52.

Kalyvas, Andreas. *Democracy and the Politics of the Extraordinary: Max Weber, Carl Schmitt, and Hannah Arendt.* Cambridge: Cambridge University Press, 2008.

"Kant, The Autonomy Formula." https://plato.stanford.edu/entries/kant-moral/#AutFor

Kelly, George Armstrong. "Rousseau, Kant, and History." *Journal of the History of Ideas* 29, no. 3 (1968): 347–64. https://doi.org/10.2307/2708447

Kettunen, Pauli. "The Rise and Fall of the Nordic Utopia of an Egalitarian Wage Work Society." In *The Relational Nordic Welfare State: Between Utopia and Ideology.*

Edited by Kirsi Lehtelä, Sakari Hänninen and Paula Saikkonen, 95–118. London, UK: Edward Elgar, 2019.

Koselleck, Reinhart. *The Practice of Conceptual History: Timing History, Spacing Concepts. Cultural Memory in the Present.* Translated by Hayden White. Stanford, CA: Stanford University Press, 2002.

Laval, Christian, in interview. http://seer.upf.br/index.php/rep/article/view/12804; https://doi.org/10.5335/rep.v28i1.12804

Laval, Christian, and Francis Vergne. *Éducation Démocratique: La Révolution Scolaire À Venir.* Paris: La Découverte, 2021.

Losito, Bruno, Gabriella Agrusti, Valeria Damiani and Wolfram Schulz. "Main Findings." In *Young People's Perceptions of Europe in a Time of Change: IEA International Civic and Citizenship Education Study 2016 European Report.* Cham: Springer Open, 2018. https://doi.org/10.1007/978-3-319-73960-1_5

Løvlie, Lars, and Paul Standish. "Introduction: Bildung and the Idea of a Liberal Education." *Journal of Philosophy of Education* 36, no. 3 (2002): 317–40.

Mickenberg, Julia L. *Learning from the Left: Children's Literature, the Cold War, and Radical Politics in the United States.* Oxford: Oxford University Press, 2006.

Mouffe, Chantal. *The Return of the Political.* London: Verso, 1993.

Mouffe, Chantal. *On the Political. Thinking in Action.* London: Routledge, 2005.

NORAD: The Norwegian Agency for Development Cooperation, "The Right to Education." https://www.norad.no/en/front/thematic-areas/education/right-to-education/, accessed 13 August 2022.

Nordhagen, Vebjørn. *Social Inequality and Political Disengagement Social Class and The Sense of Entitlement to Have an Opinion.* Master thesis in sociology. Department of Sociology and Human Geography, University of Oslo, 2019.

Nussbaum, Martha C. *Not for Profit: Why Democracy Needs the Humanities.* The Public Square Book Series. Princeton, NJ: Princeton University Press, 2010.

Ober, Josiah. *The Athenian Revolution: Essays on Ancient Greek Democracy and Political Theory.* Princeton, NJ: Princeton University Press, 1996.

OECD. http://norden.diva-portal.org/smash/record.jsf?pid=diva2%3A1198429&dswid=-2405

Oettingen, Alexander Von. *Det Pædagogiske Paradoks: Et Grundstudie i Almen Pædagogik.* Århus: Klim, 2001.

Olsen, Mark, and Michael A. Peters. "Neoliberalism, Higher Education and the Knowledge Economy: From the Free Market to Knowledge Capitalism." *Journal of Education Policy* 20 no. 3 (2005): 313–45.

Packer, George. *Last Best Hope: America in Crisis and Renewal.* New York: Farrar, Straus and Giroux, 2021.

Paolantonio, Mario Di. "The Cruel Optimism of Education and Education's Implication with 'Passing-on.'" *Journal of Philosophy of Education* 50, no. 2 (2016): 147–59.

Papastephanou, Marianna. "Philosophical Presuppositions of Citizenship Education and Political Liberalism." In *The SAGE Handbook of Education for Citizenship and Democracy,* 40–56. London: SAGE Publications, 2008.

Papastephanou, Marianna. "Genocide, Diversity and John Dewey's Progressive Education." *Metaphilosophy* 47, nos. 4–5 (October 2016). http://www.jaas.gr.jp/jjas/PDF/2007/No.18-107.pdf

Papastephanou, Marianna "What Lies within Gert Biesta's Going Beyond Learning?" *Ethics and Education* 15, no. 3 (2020): 275–99. https://doi.org/10.1080/17449642.2020.1774722

Peters, Richard Stanley. "Education as Initiation." In *Philosophy of Education: An Anthology*. Edited by Randall Curren, 55–67. Oxford: Blackwell, 2007.

Petras, James. "The CIA and the Cultural Cold War Revisited." *Monthly* Review 51, no. 6 (November 1999). https://monthlyreview.org/1999/11/01/the-cia-and-the-cultural-cold-war-revisited/

Piketty, Thomas. *Capital in the Twenty-First Century*. Translated by Arthur Goldhammer. London: Harvard/Belknap, 2014.

Pring, Richard. "Philosophical Issues in Educational Research: An Overview." In *Encyclopedia of Educational Theory and Philosophy, Vol. 2*. Edited by D. C. Phillips, 616–21. Thousand Oaks, CA: SAGE, 2014.

Raaflaub, Kurt A., Robert W. Wallace, and Josiah Ober. *Origins of Democracy in Ancient Greece*. The Joan Palevsky Imprint in Classical Literature. Berkeley: University of California Press, 2007.

Rawls, John. *Political Liberalism*, expanded edition. New York, Columbia, 2005.

Robertson, Susan L., and Matias Nestore. "Education Cleavages, or Market Society and the Rise of Authoritarian Populism?" *Globalisation, Societies and Education* 20, no. 2 (2022): 110–23 [in my pdf, 1-14]. https://doi.org/10.1080/14767724.2021.1955662

Rømer, Thomas Aastrup. "Gert Biesta – Education between Bildung and Post-structuralism." *Educational Philosophy and Theory* 53, no. 1 (2021): 34–45.

Rosa, Hartmut. *Alienation and Acceleration: Towards a Critical Theory of Late-Modern Temporality*. Vol. 3. NSU Summertalk. Malmö: NSU Press, 2010.

Rosa, Hartmut "Dynamic Stabilization, the Triple A. Approach to the Good Life, and the Resonance Conception" *Questions de communication* [online], 31 | 2017, published September 1 2019, accessed February 23 2023. URL: http://journals.openedition.org/questionsdecommunication/11228 ; DOI: https://doi.org/10.4000/questionsdecommunication.11228.

Rosanvallon, Pierre. "The Political Theory of Democracy." In *Pierre Rosanvallon's Political Thought*. Edited by Oliver Flügel-Martinsen, Franziska Martinsen, Stephen W. Sawyer and Daniel Schulz. Bielefeld: Bielefeld University Press, transcript, 2018. https://doi.org/10.14361/9783839446522-003

Ruitenberg, Claudia W. "Educating Political Adversaries: Chantal Mouffe and Radical Democratic Citizenship Education." *Studies in Philosophy and Education* 28, no. 3 (2008): 269–81.

Sagoff, Mark. *The Economy of the Earth: Philosophy, Law, and the Environment*. Cambridge Studies in Philosophy and Public Policy. Cambridge: Cambridge University Press, 1988.

Saltman, Kenneth J. "Artificial Intelligence and the Technological Turn of Public Education Privatization: In Defence of Democratic Education." *London Review of Education* 18, no. 2 (2020): 196.

Sandel, Michael. *The Tyranny of Merit. What's Become of the Common Good?* New York: Farrar, Straus and Giroux, 2020.

Simons, Maarten, and Jan Masschelein. "The Governmentalization of Learning and the Assemblage of a Learning Apparatus." *Educational Theory* 58, no. 4 (2008): 391–415.

Sinnes, Astrid. *Action, Takk! Hva kan skolen lære av unge menneskers handlinger?* Oslo: Gyldendal, 2020.

Skinner, Burrhus Fredrick. *Walden Two*, revised edition. New York: Macmillan, 1976.

Spring, Joel. *The Politics of American Education*. New York/London: Routledge, 2011.

Stockholm Resilience Centre. https://www.stockholmresilience.org/research/planetary-boundaries.html, accessed 5 August 2022.

Straume, Ingerid S. "'Learning' and Signification in Neoliberal Governance." In *Depoliticization: The Political Imaginary of Global Capitalism*. Edited by Ingerid S. Straume and John F. Humphrey, 229–59. Aarhus: NSU Press, 2011.

Straume, Ingerid S. (ed.). *Danningens filosofihistorie*. Oslo: Gyldendal, 2013

Straume, Ingerid S. "Bildung from Paideia to the Modern Subject." In *Oxford Research Encyclopedia of Education*. Edited by Kathy Hytten. 27 August 2020. https://oxfordre.com/education/view/10.1093/acrefore/9780190264093.001.0001/acrefore-9780190264093-e-1417

Szkudlarek, Tomasz. *On the Politics of Educational Theory. Rhetoric, Theoretical Ambiguity, and the Construction of Society*. New York: Routledge, 2016.

Taylor, Charles. *Human Agency and Language. Philosophical Papers*. Cambridge: Cambridge University Press, 1985.

Tiainen, Katariina, Anniina Leiviskä and Kristiina Brunila. "Democratic Education for Hope: Contesting the Neoliberal Common Sense." *Studies in Philosophy and Education* 38, no. 6 (2019): 641–55.

Topolovčan, Tomislav, and Snjezana Dubovicki. "The Heritage of the Cold War in Contemporary Curricula and Educational Reforms." *CEPS Journal* 9, no. 2 (2019): 11–32. https://doi.org/10.26529/cepsj.567

Tröhler, Daniel. "The Technocratic Momentum after 1945, the Development of Teaching Machines, and Sobering Results." *Journal of Educational Media, Memory, and Society* 5, no. 2 (2013): 1–19.

Tröhler, Daniel. "Introduction: The Nordic Education Model: Trajectories, Configurations, Challenges." In *The Nordic Education Model in Context: Historical Developments and Current Renegotiations*. Edited by Daniel Tröhler, Bernadette Hörmann, Sverre Tveit and Inga Bostad, 1–12. London: Routledge, 2022.

Tröhler, Daniel, Bernadette Hörmann, Sverre Tveit and Inga Bostad (eds.). *The Nordic Education Model in Context: Historical Developments and Current Renegotiations*. London: Routledge, 2022.

Universal Declaration of Human Rights (UDHR). https://www.un.org/en/about-us/universal-declaration-of-human-rights

Urbinati, Nadia. *Me the People: How Populism Transforms Democracy.* Cambridge, MA: Harvard University Press, 2019.

Varieties of Democracy. https://www.v-dem.net/

Westbury, Ian, Stefan Hopmann and Kurt Riquarts. *Teaching as a Reflective Practice: The German Didaktik Tradition.* Studies in Curriculum Theory. Mahwah, NJ: Lawrence Erlbaum Associates, 2012.

Wiley, James. *Politics and the Concept of the Political. The Political Imagination.* New York: Routledge, 2016.

Wolin, Sheldon S. *Politics and Vision: Continuity and Innovation in Western Political Thought,* expanded edition. Princeton, NJ: Princeton University Press, 2004.

Yaylaci, Filiz. "Analysis of Suicides Related with Educational Failure." *The Anthropologist* 19, no. 2 (2015): 507–16. https://doi.org/10.1080/09720073.2015.11891685

Zuboff, Shoshana. *The Age of Surveillance Capitalism: The Fight for the Future at the New Frontier of Power.* London: Profile Books PublicAffairs, 2019.

Index

subject positions: the entrepreneur, 15, 23, 34, 65, 71, 81, 93, 126–26; of the individual, 124; neoliberal, 79, 81, 88; political, 120. *See also* citizen, role of vs. consumer
subjectification, 68, 70, 75–76, 78–80, 86n75, 88
success, 31; and failure seen as deserved, 24–26
surveillance. *See* capitalism, surveillance
sustainability: the United Nations Sustainability Goals, 17; unsustainable development, 1–2, 123, 126
Szkudlarek, Tomasz, 66, 87

Taliban, 18–20, 23
Taylor, Charles, 5, 50, 98
teachers, 21, 26, 32–33, 35–37, 41, 55, 59, 60, 61, 63, 66–67, 71–74; teacher-student relationship, 80, 85n61
teaching machine, 29, 30, 34–36
testing, 10, 23, 26, 30, 66; of abilities, 29; assessment, 35, 37n2; benchmarking, 26, 33, 71; educational-psychological, 30, 39n52
textbooks, 16, 32
Trump, Donald, 90, 112, 117n62, 120
trust, 8–9, 42, 61, 92, 120; distrust, 9, 82, 120

Thunberg, Greta, 121–22

the United Nations' Sustainability Goals. *See* sustainability
Universal Declaration of Human Rights, 17–18
the university, 11, 18–20, 24–25, 31, 33–34, 61, 70, 109, 125; in Europe, 8–9, 44–49
the United States, 7–8, 19, 22, 24–28, 30–31, 33, 35, 39n52, 43–44, 90, 117n62, 120, 122; the National Defense Education Act of 1958, 27. *See also* educational systems
the USSR. *See* the Soviet Union

V-Dem (The Varieties of Democracy Research Project), 92, 115n18.
Vergne, Francis, 5, 124, 126
Vygotsky, Lev, 73, 85n60

Western societies and culture, 2, 32–33, 42, 52, 88, 96; westernisation, 18, 20–22, 37n8,
Whitehead, Alfred North, 63
Williams, Raymond, 65
Wolin, Sheldon, 104

Zuboff, Shoshana, 34

~

About the Author

Ingerid S. Straume is a Norwegian philosopher of education. Her research is mostly interdisciplinary, spanning political and educational thought related to questions such as environmental politics, climate change and depoliticisation of the public sphere. In her doctoral thesis, she explored the educational relevance of Cornelius Castoriadis's theory, especially his notion of a political *paideia* related to individual and collective autonomy and the social imaginary (title: *Politikken og det imaginære: Cornelius Castoriadis' bidrag til en politisk danningsteori / Politics and the Imaginary: Cornelius Castoriadis's Contribution to a Theory of Political Bildung*, University of Oslo, 2010).

Straume has published numerous articles, book chapters and two monographs in Norwegian: *En menneskeskapt virkelighet: klimaendring, sosiale forestillinger og pedagogisk filosofi* (*Anthropogenic Reality: Climate Change, Social Imaginaries and Philosophy of Education*, Res Publica, 2017) and *Skriveren og teksten: Fortellinger om identitet og faglig skriving* (*The Writer and the Text: Narratives about Identity and Disciplinary Writing*, NOASP Cappelen Damm, 2019). She is also the editor of five anthologies, including *Depoliticization: The Political Imaginary of Global Capitalism* (with J. F. Humphrey, NSU Press, 2011) and *Creation, Rationality and Autonomy: Essays on Cornelius Castoriadis* (with Giorgio Baruchello, Aarhus University Press, NSU, 2013), and a member of the editorial advisory board for the *International Journal of Social Imaginaries* (Brill).

Ingerid Straume is professor of education at Western Norway University of Applied Sciences. At the time this book was written, she was Director of the Academic Writing Centre at the University of Oslo Library.